I0134166

WWII

Was Britain

Right to Fight?

Robert Perks

Professor Robert Perks

Lytham St Annes

r.w.p@btinternet.com

First published in Great Britain as a softback original in 2016

Copyright © Robert Perks

The moral right of this author has been asserted.

All rights reserved.

No part of this publication may be reproduced, stored in a retrieval system, or transmitted, in any form or by any means, without the prior permission in writing of the publisher, nor be otherwise circulated in any form of binding or cover other than that in which it is published and without a similar condition including this condition being imposed on the subsequent purchaser.

Typeset in Amasis MT

Editing, typesetting and publishing by UK Book Publishing

UK Book Publishing is a trading name of Consilience Media

www.ukbookpublishing.com

ISBN: 978-1-910223-65-9

Contents

Hitler and the Nazis were responsible for deliberately murdering (exterminating) six million Jews and many others. Nothing in this book is intended in any way to justify or explain that evil. Criticism of the war, and of Churchill, do not constitute a defence of Hitler.

Dedication

To all those brave soldiers and others of previous generations who thought that it was Right to Fight.

Never in the field of human conflict was so much sacrificed by so many for so little.

To all those of future generations who oppose organised killing, warmongers and propaganda, the armaments manufacturers and the arms race; and who work for international peace, negotiation and cooperation.

Preface

I was born at the end of WW2 and so have no direct memory of it. I grew up in the shadow of the war: deaths and destruction; bombed out buildings seemed to be almost everywhere; dereliction, shortages and rationing. Nearly 800 airfields and RAF bases were constructed around the UK (about as many as there are Marks and Spencer stores today: one nearly everywhere), many as offensive bombing bases, and there are still about 20,000 pillbox defensive structures around Britain. Worse still was the legacy: wars have been justified then, and many more recently, as Good against Evil. My parents thought that war was a good thing, that WW2 was justified, and that 'we' had won. Much of what we had lost, and what it had cost, was clear for all to see. I never found out what we had won. At school I learned Religious Knowledge but I never found a religion that justified carpet bombing of cities and killing uninvolved children, women and the elderly. Nor did I ever understand why we went to war. I hope that this book answers that question.

My parents were not particularly wicked. They simply accepted conventional wisdom, myths and propaganda. They were in no position to challenge them. Perhaps the Iraq War (2003) has taught us not to accept at face value what politicians tell us.

Introduction

Do you believe all that you have been told about the Second World War (WW2, 1939-45)? Was it really Britain's finest hour? Was it simply Good (Britain and America) against Evil (Germany)? Was Britain really 'alone'? Did Britain really have no choice?

Yes, the Nazis were evil. But that does not mean that Britain and America were good. It was a major war with all the attendant evils – bombing, killing, maiming, destruction, lies and propaganda on BOTH sides.

Hitler had to be stopped, the story goes. But declaring war on Germany did not stop anything – it made matters worse. Millions of Jews were murdered. The emigration of Jews from Germany was severely restricted or prevented. The war did not help them.

It was Britain and France that declared war on Germany. Germany responded by attacking France (incredibly successfully!) and with threats to invade Britain. The declaration of war provoked him to invade territories in which he had no interest – except self-defence. Hitler wanted friendship and alliance with Britain – not war.

But Hitler went on to invade (and befriend) much of Eastern Europe – in which Britain had no interest, and no hope of being militarily effective. The idea that Britain could or should determine what happens in Eastern Europe is ludicrous. Britain thought that it was 'right' for Britain to rule over 'inferior' races in Africa and Asia. But it was 'wrong' for Germany to rule over 'inferior' Slavs in Eastern Europe.

The Law of Unintended Consequences applied to the War of Unintended Consequences. Britain and America (the 'Allies' – and they have been ever since) fought to keep that wicked dictator Hitler

i

from conquering Eastern Europe. Instead, the wicked dictator Stalin conquered most of Eastern Europe. Most, perhaps all, wars have unintended consequences.

Many Britons nostalgically wrap themselves in a blanket of self-congratulatory glory, remembering Britain's finest hour, and that Britain stood alone in the fight for freedom, democracy and Christian civilisation against the Germans.

But Britain was not 'alone'. That is a myth. She had very substantial support from the Empire. India provided more help than France ever did. There was also help from Canada, Australia, New Zealand, South Africa and many others.

During the war, freedom and democracy were suspended in Britain, and few Christians or civilised people would defend the many war crimes (eg the Allied bombing and destruction of Dresden) that inevitably followed.

Other myths, that are widely believed, include the following:

1. Germany unjustifiably invaded Poland, an unfortunate, innocent victim.
2. Britain had to help Poland because she (with France) had guaranteed Polish territorial integrity.
3. Hitler threatened to invade Britain and so we had to defend ourselves.
4. Germany bombed British cities and so we had to retaliate.
5. Churchill was a democratically elected war leader; Hitler had seized power illegitimately.
6. WW2 was a fight of Good (Britain, France, Poland, Russia, America) against Bad (Germany and the Axis powers).
7. Britain (and America) had to fight to save the Jews from the Holocaust.

8. There was little opposition to the war in Britain. The war united the country.
9. Hitler was the aggressor who conquered most of Europe and would have conquered the world. He had to be stopped. Churchill preferred 'jaw jaw' to 'war war' but had no choice but to continue with the war.
10. Germany had invaded Czechoslovakia, Poland, Norway and France. Britain had to stand up to her.
11. The war was necessary to save the (British) Empire.
12. Britain (ie Churchill!) won the war.

However, it is increasingly recognised that most of the above is either misleading or simply untrue. The British Empire ruled over many millions of what Churchill and others thought of as inferior races throughout the world – and that was acceptable. But it was not acceptable for Germany to rule anyone, and she was not allowed to threaten Britain's belief in her own supremacy – and superiority.

1. Germany had some justification for invading Poland, and Poland was not an unfortunate innocent victim. Poland had been part of Germany and Russia for a hundred years. It did not become an independent country until twenty years previously at the vindictive Versailles treaty which was imposed on Germany in 1919. Hitler was popular in Germany partly because he was reversing that treaty and dealing with the provocations of a Polish corridor having being imposed which divided Germany into two parts. Germany had a very good claim to Danzig (95% German), and there were many Germans in the Polish Corridor. Poland did not treat its minorities well, was as guilty as others of seizing territory, and was unreasonably intransigent in negotiations. Poland was so frightened of negotiating with its neighbours that it ended up being invaded by both. Poland is dealt with in more detail in Chapter 3.

2. Britain had not guaranteed the territorial integrity of Poland, and would have accepted German occupation of some territory (that was currently Polish, previously German) to avoid war. Poland would concede nothing. Britain had guaranteed Polish independence, but did nothing to help them when Germany (then Russia) invaded. The guarantee did not help Poland. Poland was hopelessly defeated by Germany and Russia. Britain's promise was worth no more than Germany's.

3. Hitler wanted Britain as an ally. It was not until AFTER Britain had declared war on Germany that a German invasion was even a possibility. Britain's declaration of war provoked that possibility. It is not even clear that Churchill really believed that Germany would invade Britain. Hitler's threats, and the Battle of Britain, may all have been a diversion to divert the Soviets from Hitler's plan to invade them.

4. It is not really clear who started the bombing of civilians in cities. Hitler certainly used such bombing to support his military invasions, and the Germans 'accidentally' dropped a bomb on London early in the war. Britain started bombing German cities soon after Churchill was appointed, and it was several months before Germany began to retaliate. It is clear, however, that Britain (and America –'the Allies') inflicted far more (at least eight times as much) bomb damage on Germany than Germany inflicted on Britain. British histories are full of accounts of the dreadful damage done by German bombing to British cities. They have much less to say about the far worse damage that was inflicted on Germany by the Allies.

5. Churchill was not a democratically elected war leader. He was appointed Prime Minister by the King on the advice of the previous Prime Minister (Chamberlain) although both would have preferred Halifax. Hitler was legitimately elected and

appointed. Churchill did not stand for election as Prime Minister until after the war when he lost (1945 and 1950). He did not 'win' until 1951, and even then the Labour Party won more votes than his Conservative Party did. He had a low opinion of ordinary voters, and his democratic credentials are weak – except that he always maintained the support of the House of Commons (if not the People). Chapter 4 outlines Churchill's career.

6. When Chamberlain declared war on Germany, he did so in terms of Good versus Evil (Chapter 6). Hitler had not kept his word over Czechoslovakia. But Britain did not keep her word when she promised disarmament, and to defend Poland. Hitler's regime was evil: so was that of Britain's allies Poland and Russia. Even Britain and America were not as saintly as they might have preferred to believe.

7. Britain and America did little or nothing to save the Jews from the Holocaust – indeed it had not even begun (and was not even thought of) until AFTER Britain declared war on Germany. Britain certainly blocked Jews from going to Palestine, and the declaration of war may well have done the Jews more harm than good: it made Jewish emigration from Germany almost impossible (for example it stopped the Kindertransport) and may well have provoked Hitler into more extreme anti-Semitism. Britain's declaring war on Germany did not cause the Holocaust, but it did nothing to help the Jews or to prevent the Holocaust. It was 'secret' – but the British Government knew (See Chapter 5, Part 5).

8. It is difficult to judge the amount of opposition to the war that existed in Britain as freedom of speech was suspended, and criticism of the war, or defeatism, were not allowed. There was certainly much opposition to the war at first, not least from leading aristocrats, business people, and the Royal Family. For

many, the Soviets, not the Nazis, were the real enemy. There were important conscientious objectors. There was no General Election after 1935, and by-elections were not contested by the main parties, leaving the incumbent party with a free run. But the government sometimes had difficulty retaining seats with pro-war candidates.

9. Churchill was a warmonger who wanted to continue with the war although Hitler made several offers of peace. The suggestion that Hitler wanted to conquer the world was largely American propaganda to persuade the reluctant American public to support the war. Hitler conquered France, and the Low Countries en route, because the French had declared war on Germany. He conquered Norway, and Denmark en route, to protect his iron ore supplies, and because Britain was about to invade Norway. Many of Germany's early advances were provoked by Britain and France declaring war on Germany. Others were to regain territory lost at the Treaty of Versailles. Russia, at the beginning of the war, was Germany's ally. After taking large chunks of Poland, the Soviets seized Latvia, Lithuania and Estonia, parts of Romania and won territorial concessions from Finland. In many ways the Russians were as bad as the Germans. But Russia became an ally of Britain and America, while Germany remained the enemy.

10. It seems that Hitler over-stepped the mark in taking over the failing state of Czechoslovakia. He had a better case with Poland, and Britain had been willing to negotiate. His interests were in Eastern, not Western Europe. But Britain had planned to invade Norway – so Hitler did it first. He invaded France to protect his western front because France had first declared war on Germany.

11. The war did not save the Empire. Instead, it bankrupted Britain and contributed to the demise of the Empire.

12. Britain did not win anything. The Soviets defeated Germany and won most of Eastern Europe for themselves. The British assisted with the American invasion from the west. Germany lost, the Soviets won (at the cost of many lives), America came second, Britain was bankrupted. But Churchill won the propaganda war.

So why did it all happen? There were many contributory factors:

- The manufacturers of armaments, vehicles and many others do well out of wars, and even supply both sides in a conflict. The American People did not want to join in WW2, but they were persuaded to participate by powerful interest groups who painted the Germans in the darkest possible shades.
- Britain thought she could maintain some sort of 'balance of power' in Europe, and perhaps even thought that she could and should rule the waves, and much of the world.
- Churchill was well aware of the reputation, gained through war in Europe, of his ancestor Marlborough, and sought to emulate him. He wanted to, and did, become widely acclaimed as the greatest man in the world, and the saviour of civilisation and democracy. Churchill personally, the Soviet Government, and American manufacturers seemed to be the only winners in the war. Everyone else made major sacrifices.
- Hitler was indeed wicked – as were some of Britain's main allies. Despite the Allies' efforts, it was Hitler who managed to kill Hitler.
- Hitler's warmongering and aggression may have been exaggerated, but were certainly a factor, as was his determination to reverse many of the humiliating and vindictive provisions of the Treaty of Versailles.

Read on if you dare. Prepare to be challenged and to feel uncomfortable. Feel free to disagree, to check the things that I have said. Some, even friends, believe that I should not have written such a book. But please try to consider the issues with an open mind, and in light of the world today.

Outline of Book

Chapter 1 provides a brief overview of WW2 for those who have little or no knowledge of it. It includes a chart, or time-line for easy reference. More detail is provided in subsequent chapters, particularly regarding Europe and the beginnings of WW2.

Chapter 2 outlines the origins of WW2, summarising the provisions of the Treaty of Versailles, the origins of Hitler, and how the treaty was steadily derailed.

Chapter 3 deals with Poland, which was central to the outbreak of war.

Chapter 4 is an outline of the career of Churchill before he became Prime Minister, and how good fortune and careful manoeuvring enabled him to become a War Leader.

Chapter 5 assumes that war was not inevitable and examines what alternatives to war there were in 1939-40. Many different policies were possible, depending on which objectives were to be pursued.

Chapter 6 deals with the war under Chamberlain 1939-40 and how events led to Churchill becoming Prime Minister.

Chapter 7 is about Churchill's beginning as a War Leader, the events immediately afterwards, and the possible existence of a 'peace party', particularly in relation to Rudolf Hess's trip, and to the Duke of Kent's death.

Chapter 8 outlines the consequences of WW2 in deaths, destruction, injuries, resources, and Britain's position in the world, and also refers to some positive consequences.

Chapter 9 deals with the morality of war generally, and the Christian concept of a 'just war'.

Chapter 10 examines some of the myths about WW2, and makes some generalisations about wars.

Chapter 1
Outline of WW2

WW2 was fought between

1. The Allies: Britain and most of the Empire, France until it surrendered in June 1940, Russia from July 1941, America from December 1941; and
2. Germany, and the territories it controlled, and the Axis Powers, Italy and Japan.

This book is primarily concerned with the war in Europe, rather than the rest of the world. The war is often presented as being Britain (Churchill) and the Allies against Hitler and Nazism. Hitler is usually presented as the Evil One – which he was. But the Allies included Stalin – also an Evil One. And America and Britain were far from being Saints in the conduct of the war.

The First World War (WW1 1914-18/19) ended with the Treaty of Versailles in which the vindictive victors humiliated Germany. It could be argued that WW2 was a continuation of WW1.

Hitler came to power in 1933, determined to reverse that treaty and to restore Germany to her rightful place as a great nation.

The Treaty had created Czechoslovakia, a strange mixture of a country, which included the (German) Sudetenland. Germany wanted it back, and crisis and war threatened. Chamberlain, and most of Britain, wanted peace, and so 'Appeasement' followed with the Munich Treaty which gave Hitler what he wanted. But he took more.

Britain and France wanted to stop Germany from expanding and so they gave the foolish[1] Polish Guarantee. Hitler (rightly) assumed that it was a bluff and invaded Poland on September 1, 1939, in collusion with Russia. The situation that existed before the Treaty of Versailles was restored and WW2 had begun. Britain and France declared war on Germany. The 'Phoney War' followed which included some nasty naval engagements, but little happened on land. The British Army was soon surrounded at Dunkirk. On May 24-25, 1940 the Germans could easily have destroyed the British Expeditionary Force. The BEF was retreating to Dunkirk, hotly pursued by the Germans. But Hitler told his army to stop. Whether that was incompetence, a mistake, or kindness, we may never know. It seems that, at that stage, Hitler wanted to be friendly with Britain. He hoped for an alliance, or at least neutrality, while he pushed into Eastern Europe. The BEF was forced to retreat and was evacuated by whatever ships and boats could be found.

The 'Battle of Britain' took place soon afterwards (July-September 1940). Germany attacked British airfields from the air, trying and failing to gain superiority in the air. Hitler offered peace to Britain, saying he had no desire to destroy the British Empire, but Churchill preferred war.

Shortly after the invasion of Poland, the French ordered a small attack on Saarland, intended to divert German troops from Poland; but it soon fizzled out and no German troops were diverted. The French army was soon on the run. France was defeated and surrendered within 10 months.

Churchill, then First Lord of the Admiralty, was organising an invasion of neutral Norway, to cut off Swedish iron ore supplies to Germany. But it was an incompetent muddle, and Germany got there first, invading Denmark and Norway. Britain then invaded Iceland

---

1   See Chapter 3

and the Faroes to stop Germany getting there first.

Hitler had always made it clear that he wanted to expand eastwards and to be some sort of 'overlord' over what he regarded as inferior races there. He would see it as being comparable with Britain's Empire, ruling over inferior races in Asia and Africa. He was not interested in Western Europe, but once France had declared war on Germany, he had to defend Germany's western front.

Because of the incompetent 'invasion' of Norway, Chamberlain resigned as Prime Minister, and Churchill was appointed to replace him – on May 10, 1940. On the same day Germany invaded France, attacking the Low Countries en route.

The British did not directly fight again in central and western Europe until the end of the war. They never went to Poland. They fought in the Balkans and in North Africa, eventually winning at El Alamein (Egypt). The tide began to turn against Germany. The Allies advanced through North Africa, across Sicily, through the soft underbelly of Europe, then through Italy towards Germany.

In Italy Mussolini had become a fascist dictator and had invaded Ethiopia in 1935. In June 1940 Italy joined the war on Germany's side and declared war on France and Britain. Mussolini (Italy) joined in the invasion of France, then attacked Malta, and British-held Egypt and Somaliland, and then Greece. Hitler came to Mussolini's aid, and the war soon spread to Greece and North Africa.

In September 1940 a formal alliance was concluded between the Axis Powers, Germany, Italy and Japan. It was soon joined by Hungary, Slovakia and Romania.

In 1939 Italy annexed Albania. They entered the war in June 1940, invading part of France, and declaring war on France and Britain.

They advanced on British Somalia and Egypt. They also invaded Greece, without much success, but Germany came to their aid both in Europe and in North Africa. Early in 1941 they suffered heavy defeats, particularly in North Africa. In August/September 1942, following (British) Montgomery's victory at El Alamein, the war started to turn in the Allies' favour; they advanced westwards across North Africa. In July 1943 the Allies (USA and Britain) invaded Sicily, and began to advance through Italy from the south. Although Mussolini fell (July 1943) and Italy surrendered (September 1943), the Germans continued to occupy central and northern Italy until April 1945.

Meanwhile trouble continued in the Far East, making it genuinely a World War. There had long been hostilities between Japan and China. In 1931 Japan had invaded Manchuria, and the Second Sino-Japanese War began in July 1937. But in the Far East WW2 is usually seen as beginning in December 1941 when Japan invaded Thailand, attacked the British possessions of Singapore, Malaya and Hong Kong, and the American naval bases in Pearl Harbour (Hawaii) and the Philippines. For the first couple of years the Japanese were overwhelmingly successful, invading Burma, the Dutch East Indies, New Guinea, the Solomon Islands, Bali, Timor and attacking Northern Australia and launching a submarine attack on Sydney Harbour. They were powerful on land, sea and air and threatened to isolate Australia, until they were forced to abandon this after the Battle of the Coral Sea (May 1942). The Allied fightback had begun and became more effective after the Cairo Conference (Nov 1943; it included US President Roosevelt, Churchill and Chiang Kai-Shek[2]). But the Japanese fought back, particularly in India and China, and their defeat, one territory at a time, came slowly in 1944-5, until their final surrender after the Allies dropped atomic bombs in Nagasaki and Hiroshima. V-J (Victory in Japan) day was August 14, 1945.

---

2   1887-1975, leader of the Republic of China 1928-75

The Americans, with British help, carried out the Normandy Landings on 6 June 1944 (D-Day) and advanced eastwards towards Germany. Meanwhile, the Soviets were advancing westwards into Germany.

Most of the concentration camps, where more than six million Jews and others had been systematically murdered, were liberated in the first half of 1945, by the Soviets, and then the Americans and the British. The horrors of the Holocaust then came to be widely known and provided a convenient justification for the Allies' participation in the war, and then for the trial and execution of leading Nazis after the Nuremberg Trials (November 1945-October 1946).

Most British people remembered the evidence of these trials, and the wickedness of the Nazis. They could feel it was all worthwhile; Hitler could not be left to murder millions of Jews. They conveniently forgot that Britain entered the war to save Poland, but they failed to do so. Britain did not enter the war to save the Jews, however much they subsequently thought they did. And they did not save, or attempt to save, six million Jews.

The Second World War was one of the biggest and worst things to happen in British history: in casualties (injuries and deaths); in destruction, including homes and infrastructure; and financially – Britain incurred crippling burdens and became a debtor nation. Some would argue that the war led directly to the loss of Empire (Buchanan, 2008). Britain became a second rate power, apparently subservient to the USA. Moreover, it changed attitudes to war. After the horrors of the First World War (WW1 1914-1918)[3], pacifism became a respectable cause. But, after WW2, for most people,

---

3   WW1 was labelled by some, eg Sellar and Yeatman (p 121) as the 'Great War to End War'. It was totally unsuccessful in ending war. It was concluded with the Peace to End Peace – which was totally successful!

'Pacifism' and 'Appeasement' were discredited. War seemed to be justified. A generation later, in the light of the Vietnam War, young people were urged to 'Make Love Not War'. But wars continued, as if they were justified, often, it seemed, with the aim of total victory and total defeat, destruction and humiliation of the opponent.

Most people born before about 1955 grew up in the shadow of WW2, remembering (or with their parents remembering) the suffering and sacrifices – and the myths – of WW2. They are unlikely to abandon the myths with which they grew up, and many continue to believe that Britain was right to fight. Perhaps they will always believe that wars can be justifiable. That attitude will lead to the next world war which will destroy us all.

Younger people are more likely to believe that WW2 was so long ago that we should now move on and forget about it. That is how I regard Napoleon and his wars. But younger people should see the continuing relevance of WW2 today, in the following ways:

1. It confirmed the British-American alliance, and provided a justification for many subsequent wars and bombing campaigns that were supposedly Good versus Evil.
2. It meant that Britain spent far too much money on warmongering rather than (for example) housebuilding. The current housing crisis would not have happened if 1930s housebuilding had continued (instead of houses being bombed and destroyed). If money spent on the war had been spent on housebuilding, there would be no housing crisis today.
3. Before the war started, the myth was that it was to save Poland. After the war finished, the myth was that it was to save the Jews. It did neither, and little or no attempt was made to do either.
4. Politicians too easily believe that a war is needed and justified, without giving sufficient consideration to the horrific consequences, and the innocent victims. In turn they are able to

persuade the people, or their representatives in Parliament, of the need for action, and that Right is on their side. (Their enemies similarly believe that Right is on their side.)

The first casualty in war is Truth.

In the twenty first century the world is a much more dangerous place, especially with the spread of nuclear weapons. But the People are much more aware of what is being done in their name and are less ready to believe in politicians and their arguments for War.

YEAR(S)	MONTH/ DAY	EVENTS
1914- 1918	July 28 Nov 11	First World War Allies (UK, France, Russia; later + Italy, Japan and USA) versus Central Powers (Germany, Austria-Hungary + Ottoman Empire, Bulgaria)
1919	June 28	Treaty of Versailles, plus associated treaties, marked end of WW1 Germany humiliated, loss of territory, had to pay reparations, largely disarmed
1933	Jan 30	Hitler appointed Chancellor of Germany
1932-4	Oct	World Disarmament Conference, Geneva, fails to agree
	Oct	Germany withdraws from League of Nations
		Germany rearms; arms race begins
1935	June 18	British-German Naval Agreement, to limit size of German navy
1933- 1938		Hitler annexes various former German territories, plus Austria
1938	Sept 29	Munich Agreement: Britain, France, Italy and Germany agree to Germany's annexation of Sudetenland (part of Czechoslovakia); initially welcomed; soon discredited as 'Appeasement'.
		Czechoslovakia dismembered by Germany, Poland, and Hungary
1939	Mar 31	Britain with French support guarantee Poland's independence
1939	Sept 1	Hitler invades Poland
	Sept 3	Britain and France declare war on Germany
1939- 1940	Sept- May	'Phoney War': Serious war did not begin
	Sept 17	Russia invades Poland, in collaboration with Germany; country divided between them
1940	Apr 8	Beginning of Britain's Operation Wilfred, laying mines in neutral Norwegian territorial waters
1940	April 9	German invasion of Denmark begins
1940	May 10	German invasion of France begins, via Low Countries End of 'phoney war'
	May 10	Churchill appointed as Prime Minister
	May 10	Allied occupation of Faroes, Iceland and Greenland
	May 11	Britain starts bombing German cities

	May 20	Defence Regulation 18B(1A) enabled British Government to imprison suspected opponents at will without trial
	Jun 22	France surrenders, armistice with Germany
	Sept 7	Germany starts bombing British cities
1940	May 27-June 4	German army drives British Expeditionary Force to Channel Coast; most of them evacuated from Dunkirk by ships and boats
1940	June	Russia forcibly annexes Estonia, Latvia, Lithuania and parts of Romania
1941	May 10	Rudolf Hess flies to Britain seeking peace
	May 10-11	Extra heavy bombing of London; Parliament bombed
1941	June 22	Germany + Italy + Romania invade Russia; 'Operation Barbarossa'
1941	July	Britain and Russia form alliance against Germany
1941	Dec 7	Japanese bomb Pearl Harbor. USA enters war against Germany + Japan
1941	Dec 11	Hitler declares war on America
1942	Oct 23-Nov 11	2nd battle of El Alamein. North Africa. Allies start to turn the tide against Axis powers *This is not the end. It is not even the beginning of the end. It is perhaps the end of the beginning*
1944	June 6	D day: beginning of allied landings in Normandy. The Western Front had begun
	Jan 27	Auschwitz concentration camp liberated by Russians
	Aug 25	Paris liberated (by the French)
1945	Feb 13-15	Allies bomb Dresden
	Mar 22	Americans cross Rhine into Germany
	Apr 27	Russian forces completely surround Germans in Berlin
	Apr 29	Mussolini shot and hanged
	Apr 30	Hitler commits suicide
	May 2	Berlin surrenders
1945	May 5	V-E (Victory in Europe) Day
1945	May 8	German unconditional surrender
	Aug 6	Americans drop atomic bomb on Hiroshima, Japan
	Aug 9	Americans drop atomic bomb on Nagasaki, Japan
1945	Aug 15	V-J (Victory in Japan) Day

Chamberlain arrived at Heston Aerodrome (near Heathrow) on September 30, 1938, after meeting Hitler at Munich, waving a piece of paper saying he had brought "peace for our time". He was greeted enthusiastically by crowds who wanted Peace.

Continued welcome for Peace, in Downing Street.

Peace was welcomed by the crowds. Winston Churchill waves to crowds in Whitehall, London on the day he broadcast the news that the war with Germany was over

Crowds at Piccadilly Circus, London celebrating V-E Day and a public holiday, May 8th 1945

Chapter 2
Events Leading to War

One war often leads to another war, and, indeed, WW1 was a major cause of WW2. In particular, the Treaty of Versailles (1919), at the end of that war, was a major humiliation for Germany, which facilitated the rise of Hitler.

This chapter:

1. Summarises the provisions of that treaty;
2. Describes the origins of Adolph Hitler; and
3. Examines the causes of WW2.

1. The Treaty of Versailles (and associated treaties)

The Treaty was humiliating for Germany, and even the British had serious reservations about it. Under its provisions, Germany had to give:

1. Alsace-Lorraine to France;
2. Eupen and Malmedy to Belgium;
3. Northern Schleswig to Denmark;
4. Hultschkin to Czechoslovakia;
5. West Prussia and the corridor between East Prussia and Germany, together with the rich agricultural land of Posen (Poznan) and Upper Silesia, to Poland;
6. The Saar, with its rich coalfields, to France;
7. Danzig (was made a Free City) and Memel were placed under League of Nations control;
8. All Germany's overseas colonies were given mainly to Britain and France under League of Nations control;
9. Germany was held responsible for all damage caused by WW1,

and reparations had to be paid, eventually agreed at £6,600 million (132 billion gold marks; or US$442 billion). This was excessive, punitive and unrealistic, and much of it was never paid. The reparations contributed to Germany's hyperinflation.

10. The Treaty also established the League of Nations. America did not join. Germany was not at first allowed to join but was a member from 1926 to 1933, when it left because of the failure of disarmament negotiations.

11. Germany had to reduce its army to 100,000 men, with no tanks, and was allowed no air force, and their navy had to be reduced to six battleships and defined numbers of smaller ships, but no submarines.

12. No German soldiers or weapons were allowed within 50 km east of the Rhine, and a demilitarized zone was established west of the Rhine, occupied by allied forces for 15 years.

13. Germany was not allowed to unite with Austria.

The loss of territory around the Rhine meant a serious loss of coal production, and it all seemed (at least to German eyes) designed to prevent Germany being a great power again.

In summary:

The peace treaty had taken from Germany all its colonies, one eighth of its European territory, and one tenth of its European population, and most of its iron and steel and shipbuilding; it had placed the Rhineland and the Saar temporarily under foreign control, eliminated the German navy and air-force, and reduced the German army to a force of 100,000 men ... extracted a written admission of war guilt and imposed an obligation to pay extensive but as yet unlimited reparations.[4]

The limitations on German armed forces were justified by the

---

4   Calvocoressi, p 31

promise that other countries (including Germany's enemies) would disarm similarly. But they did not.

If general disarmament had taken place, as agreed, there may have been no general rearmament and rush to war. But many Germans wanted to regain what their country had lost, and build up stronger defence forces.

2. Adolph Hitler

Adolph Hitler was born on April 20, 1889 in Braunau am Inn, a small Austrian town on the border with Germany. His father had a successful career as a customs officer. When Adolph was three years old, his family moved to Passau in Germany. He wanted to be an artist, or perhaps an architect, but had little educational achievement. He soon adopted a German identity, criticising the mixed-race muddle of the Austro-Hungarian Empire. As a teenager, he moved to Vienna, where he was something of a drop-out, and he moved to Munich just before the First World War.

He volunteered to serve in the Bavarian army, as an Austrian citizen, and had a good war record. He was regarded as brave; he was injured and awarded medals and became a German nationalist. He was shocked that the Germans surrendered in November 1918 (the end of WW1), which he attributed to a 'stab in the back' by Germany's civilian leaders who he criticised as being Marxists and Jews; they had betrayed Germany.

He soon became a political activist and was impressed by the leader of the small German Workers Party (DAP), Anton Drexler, who was anti-Semitic, anti-capitalist, nationalist, and favoured a non-Jewish Socialism with strong, active government. Hitler developed his oratorical skills, and became an asset to the party, designing its new banner – a swastika in a white circle on a red background. The party changed its name to the National Socialist German Workers Party (NSDAP or Nazi Party). He was soon working full time for the party, and his increasingly powerful speeches and rowdy meetings were condemned by rival politicians. Hitler condemned the Treaty of Versailles, Marxists and the Jews.

There has been some speculation about the origins of his anti-Semitism, but it may be no more than that it proved to be a popular and effective line to take to help him to gain power. It was also too easy to lump Jews and Communists together and blame them for all of Germany's problems.

In 1921 there was a move to merge the NSDAP with the German Socialist Party (DSP). Hitler objected and resigned. He had become such a major asset to his party that they could not afford to let him go. Hitler announced that he would not re-join the party unless he replaced Drexler as Chairman. This was agreed, and he was given overall power and control of the party.

He was a populist and an effective, powerful speaker who was good at telling the Germans what they wanted to hear, and readily blaming Germany's troubles (defeat, loss of territory, depression, unemployment and hyper-inflation) on scapegoats, especially Marxists and Jews.

Hitler attempted a coup d'état in 1923, to take power initially in Bavaria. It failed, and 16 party members and four policemen were killed. Hitler was sentenced to five years in prison for high treason. But he was released after little more than a year. Whilst in prison he began writing *Mein Kampf,* which clearly set out his beliefs, prejudices, aims and priorities. Most of his subsequent actions were very much in line with his book, and no-one should have been surprised by what he did. Churchill had certainly studied it.

Among its assertions were:

1. Man is a fighting animal; a nation is a fighting unit. Those that cease to fight are doomed to extinction.
2. The Jewish race is necessarily pacifist and internationalist. Pacifism is the deadliest sin; it means surrendering the race in the fight for existence.
3. The New Reich must gather within its fold all the scattered German elements in Europe.
4. England and Italy are the only two possible allies for Germany.
5. Germany's lost provinces can only be regained by force of arms.
6. The world will only cease to be anti-German when Germany acquires equality of rights and resumes her place in the sun.
7. What Germany needs is an increase in territory in Europe. Germany must look for expansion to Russia and the Baltic States.
8. Germany's pre-war colonial policy was a mistake and should be abandoned.

No alliance with Russia can be tolerated. To wage war with Russia against the West would be criminal, for the aim of the Soviets is the triumph of international Judaism.

The above summary omits most of the worst anti-Semitism and ludicrous assertions (eg about the supposed superiority of the 'Aryan Race'). It does, however, make Hitler's territorial ambitions clear, and that he intended to use force of arms. He was interested in Germany's 'lost provinces', and expansion to the East (the Baltic States and towards Russia). He was not really interested in German overseas colonies in Africa and elsewhere. And he viewed 'England' as a potential ally.

No-one should have been surprised that Hitler implemented what he had always promised.

The electoral success of the Nazi Party steadily increased until 1933. The percentage of the vote which they gained in elections was as follows:

Dec	1924	3%
May	1928	2.6%
Sept	1930	18.3%
July	1932	37.3%
Nov	1932	33.1%
Mar	1933	43.9%

Hitler did not 'seize power'. He was properly appointed by the president, having several times achieved a higher proportion of the vote than many properly elected politicians in Britain receive. (In May 2015 David Cameron won a 'stunning' victory with just less than 37% of the vote.)

The Great Depression and the New York Stock Market crash were most dramatic from late 1929, and had devastating effects on Germany (and elsewhere) with banks collapsing and major unemployment. These problems followed a period of hyper-inflation in Germany in the 1920s. The Nazis were able to take advantage of this, promising to repudiate the Versailles Treaty, provide jobs, and strengthen the economy – which they did. They also gained right wing popularity because of their clear anti-Communist stance, and from blaming a lot of Germany's problems on an imaginary Jewish conspiracy. Many also opposed him: the violence at his public meetings, street fighting with communists, and the content of his speeches, outraged many, particularly liberals and left-wingers.

Hitler's anti-Semitism, his intention to overturn much of the Versailles Treaty, and to expand to the East, were clear long before he came to power.

In January 1933 Hitler was appointed as Chancellor (head of government) by President Hindenburg and, within a matter of months, he had obtained virtually dictatorial powers – almost legally. He had passed laws in the Reichstag (Parliament) increasing his powers. The Communists and some Social Democrats had been excluded, enabling him to achieve the necessary majority. When Hindenburg died in 1934, Hitler abolished the presidency, and merged the president's powers with his own; he thus became head of state as well as head of government. Other political parties were suppressed. In line with dictators everywhere, and following the tradition of Old English Kings, he also murdered ('executed') some of his enemies. His brutality was used as evidence against him by the British (who conveniently turned a blind eye to violence and murder elsewhere).

He then set about doing what he had promised. To some it might seem surprising that he actually did what he said he would do.

In March 1933, Prince Bernhard Wilhelm von Bulow (Foreign Secretary) stated the following main foreign policy aims of Germany:

1. Anschluss (unification) with Austria;
2. Restoration of Germany's 1914 borders;
3. Rejection of the military restrictions of the Treaty of Versailles;
4. Return of former German colonies in Africa;
5. A German zone of influence in Eastern Europe.

The world had been warned.

The economy was boosted with public works (eg dams, roads and railways), reconstruction and rearmament, financed by seizing assets (especially from Jews) and Meso Bills (promissory notes, much the same as borrowing). Unemployment fell from six million in 1932 to one million in 1936.

Although Hitler had recognised that war would be necessary eventually, particularly in moving into Eastern Europe, he did not want war in 1939, and certainly not with Britain. Indeed, he wanted an alliance with Britain to allow him a free hand in Eastern Europe. Besides, he had found that he could get what he wanted without war. He had already marched into:

i.   Saarland (1935)
ii. Rhineland (1936)
iii. Austria (1938)
iv. Sudetenland (the German part of Czechoslovakia, 1938)
v.   Bohemia and Moravia (much of the rest of Czechoslovakia, 1938)
vi. Eastern Czechoslovakia (1938)
vii. Memel District (Lithuania, 1939).

They were mainly German areas, mostly taken from Germany at the end of WWI. There was little opposition; fighting was avoided. Often he was welcomed. In some territories a referendum was arranged showing support for the Nazis, sometimes at 90%[5] or more. Before Czechoslovakia and Poland, and before Britain (and its Empire) and France declared war on Germany, Hitler's claims were modest and justifiable. He did not seek to regain Alsace and Lorraine, and reclaiming Saarland was exactly in accordance with the Treaty of Versailles: it was to be controlled by France for 15 years, and then there should be a plebiscite to determine its future. That is what happened.

Britain did not want war either, and Prime Minister Chamberlain had done his best to avoid it. His appeasement policies, much derided in later years, sought to accommodate Hitler. Chamberlain had flown to Germany and concluded the Munich agreement. But Hitler had affronted Chamberlain and most UK politicians by dismembering

---

5   In Saarland

the whole of Czechoslovakia, instead of limiting himself to the Sudetenland part which had been agreed. Hitler had bullied his way into Czechoslovakia, without fighting, and thought he could get away with invading Poland. He had colluded with Russia in this, and so Poland had no chance, however well they fought with their antiquated equipment. Poland reassured itself that its independence had been guaranteed by Britain and France. But the guarantee proved worthless: neither country provided any military help to Poland. Poland was conquered, and divided between Germany and Russia, restoring that country's position so that it was much as it had been before WW1.

WW2 had begun – a war which both Hitler and Chamberlain had striven to avoid. Chamberlain had gambled that, with the British and French Guarantee, Hitler would be deterred from invading. Hitler had gambled that the Guarantee was meaningless. But Britain declared war. It was all a mistake, a misunderstanding, a miscalculation.

3. Causes of WW2

Wars have many causes. In WW1 there was a spark that ignited a greater conflagration. It was the assassination of Archduke Franz Ferdinand, heir to the Austro-Hungarian throne, at Sarajevo on June 28, 1914.

In 1939 the equivalent spark was Hitler's invasion of Poland which began on September 1, 1939. Britain declared war on Germany on September 3. But there were many underlying causes.

There are the events immediately leading to the war; and there are more long-term causes of wars. The immediate causes of WW2 are usually seen as centring around the personality and aggressive attitudes of Hitler, on the unfairness of the Treaty of Versailles, and Hitler (and Germany)'s determination to undo that Treaty and to reassert Germany's pride, power and reputation.

If Hitler had not been the leader in raising national self-consciousness and resentment against Versailles, someone else would have been. There are always politicians who take advantage of whatever circumstances they find themselves in to increase their own power. Chapter 4 shows how most of Churchill's life was a preparation for such an opportunity, without which he would have been just another failed Tory MP.

There is always rivalry between nations, aided and abetted by the armaments manufacturers. We could imagine armaments manufacturers as simply being innocent bystanders, standing ready to fulfil whatever orders come their way. Or we could see them as active profit-seekers who welcome and even encourage international conflicts which boost their sales and profits. They could always point to the 'other side' having more and better weapons to encourage a country to buy more arms. The American arms industry clearly wanted to do well out of the war.

Nations may need to defend themselves against aggressors. That is self-defence. But they do not need to expand their forces and equipment and to interfere in other countries that they may not even understand. As one country expands its 'defence' capability against another, so the other feels threatened, and feels the need to expand similarly, and so an arms race ensues.

The main causes of the war may be summarised as follows:

i.   The humiliation of Germany at the end of WW1 in the Treaty of Versailles[6], and the intention of Hitler to regain much of what

---

6   Perhaps it should be labelled the 'peace treaty to end peace'. In that regard, it was totally successful.

Germany had lost;

ii. The suspicion of the Allies that Hitler would conquer more and more territory until he had conquered all of Europe, and perhaps the world;

iii. Continuing British hostility to Germany which was developed and enhanced in WW1. WW1 had been labelled the 'war to end wars'. But it was totally unsuccessful in that regard. It did not end war. It was immediately followed by a number of small wars, and then, twenty years later, by WW2. One war seems inevitably to lead to another.

iv. Border disputes. Britain is perhaps the only country in Europe with clear borders. It is an island, and the sea marks the border. In other countries the sea, or a river, or a mountain range marks some borders, but most have been a matter of continuing dispute and change over decades and centuries. At the end of WW1 some attempt was made to arrange borders around ethnic majorities. But that could not work when an area was (say) one third German, one third Czech and one third Polish. Census results were not reliable where one group of people chose to adopt a different national identity because it was to their advantage to do so. There was also the problem that thousands of people migrated to be in the country of their choice. What might seem the 'right' nation for a particular town at one time would sometimes change so that a national minority at one time became a majority a few years later. Moreover, national minorities in one area often had grievances against other national groups that dominated them. Politicians sometimes aggravated those grievances to justify intervention.

From a British perspective it may seem that countries should adhere to their 'proper' boundaries, as if there were 'proper' permanent boundaries. That is the morality of the status quo: boundaries should stay as they are. Other political leaders sought to change boundaries, where they could find an historic case, usually in their own interest. They wanted to change the status quo, and had a different morality. At the end of WW1 the American President Woodrow Wilson tried to establish correct boundaries. But he was no more successful in stopping the tides of history than Canute was in stopping the waves of the sea.

v. There were personality factors. It seems that both Churchill and Hitler were determined to have a war.

vi. There had been an arms race, as shown in the Table at the end of this chapter. Arms races are usually seen as being provocative. As one country makes more war planes, so a second country feels bound to do likewise, for 'defence'. As one country recruits and exercises more soldiers, so another country feels threatened, and fears that those soldiers may be being trained to invade; so they too need to mobilise and exercise their soldiers, thus threatening the first country.

Moreover, armaments manufacturers are always keen to sell 'better' weapons to any country. Such pressures are difficult to resist. The extent of the arms race is indicated in the figures below.[7]

vii. British foreign policy was usually based on the idea of a balance of power in Europe. No one country should be so powerful as to dominate the continent. The problem was that for decades Germany was becoming more powerful than other European countries. There was not much that Britain could do about Germany's size and population, but their manufacturing capacity

---

7   Times Atlas of WW2, 1989, p31

and natural resources were important in determining their power. The importance of manufacturing and of natural resources (especially coal, iron and oil) can be seen in the territories of which Germany was deprived in 1919, and which Germany sought to regain. But Britain was determined to stop Germany being 'top dog'.

When Churchill was a lad, Germany was a new nation; France and Britain were the powers that mattered. He could not accept the new kid on the block. When Britain and France stood together and told Germany not to invade Poland, they thought they would be obeyed. But their thinking was hopelessly out of date.

When Hitler was little more than a lad, he saw Germany being humiliated by the western powers. He was determined to reassert the power of Germany.

viii. The cruelty and tyranny of the barbaric Nazi regime was a significant factor in Britain declaring war. But it should not be exaggerated. The unbelievable excesses of the Holocaust, and murder on an industrial scale, were not known about for two years or so after the war had begun – mainly because they had not started. Kristallnacht and persecution of the Jews were known about, as were many of the violent and murderous excesses of the Nazi regime.

But most regimes in Europe were anti-Semitic, to varying degrees. Germany was probably not the worst.

Most regimes in eastern Europe were non-democratic dictatorships. Britain could not adopt the high moral ground and declare war on all of them.

Stalin's regime was far more cruel than Hitler's, especially before

1939: Stalin was responsible for far more deaths than Hitler's regime.

Anyone who claims that Britain declared war on Germany because it was a cruel and murderous tyranny, must explain why Britain did not declare war on Russia – which was worse.

Russia became Britain's ally. It is almost impossible to believe that Britain went to war with Germany because it was a cruel and murderous tyranny. Indeed, Britain seemed to think that there was nothing wrong with cruel and murderous tyrannies, provided they helped to defeat Germany. Germany must be prevented from being 'top dog' 'at all costs'.

ix. Perhaps man[8] is a fighting animal, and attempts to make the world a more civilised place need to take that on board. War itself is certainly not a civilised activity, and does not save civilisation.

The settlement at the end of WW1 was never sacrosanct. Subsequent mythology suggests that it was steadily undone by Hitler. But he was no worse than anyone else – although that changed with his occupation of Czechoslovakia and invasion of Poland; and with the declaration of war by Britain.

The Treaty of Versailles re-established the country of Poland, but it did not definitively settle the Poland-Russian border; the 'Curzon Line' was provisional. The two countries were soon fighting as Poland wanted to expand eastwards, and Russia wanted to expand westwards. After (unexpectedly) winning the Battle of Warsaw (1920), the Peace of Riga (1921) between Russia and Poland gave Poland most of the disputed territory – including chunks of western

---

8   Perhaps mankind, or perhaps men. But women can be warmongers too.

Ukraine. Poland had betrayed its Ukrainian allies, interned many Ukrainians, and assimilated non-Poles into what had become part of Poland.

The border between Poland and Czechoslovakia was also a continuing problem. For example, the area of Zaolzie (60% Polish and 25% Czech) was taken over by Poland on October 31, 1918. A few days later it was divided between Poland and Czechoslovakia. Early in 1920 Czechoslovakia invaded the whole of the area. In the summer of 1920 Czechoslovakia was given most of the area. In September 1938 Poland seized most of the area, which it held for less than a year. Eventually Germany (and Russia) took over the whole area. It seemed that borders were very uncertain, and subject to regular change. People of one ethic identity might suddenly find themselves living in a different country. At the end of WW1 the Germans of Sudetenland suddenly found themselves living in Czechoslovakia.

In 1920-22, Vilnius, the capital of the Republic of Lithuania, and the area around it, was invaded and occupied by Poland and became part of Poland.

In June 1935 Britain and Germany concluded a naval agreement whereby the German navy could be increased up to 35% of the tonnage of the British navy. This hardly suggests that Germany was planning to attack or to rival the British navy. It also shows that Britain was happy to breach the terms of the Treaty of Versailles. The agreement was made without consulting France or Italy.

The Rhineland was an important region. It was a complicated, loosely defined, and much disputed area on each side of the river Rhine between France and Germany, south of Belgium and north of Switzerland. It was an unresolved problem at the end of WW1. It was also an important part of the prologue for WW2. The area was rich in mineral wealth, and in manufacturing.

Historically, it was a loose collection of small, independent states. It was French-controlled under Napoleon until 1814. The Rhenish Province then became part of Prussia (which itself became the main part of Germany). In WW1 it was occupied by America, French, Belgian and British forces. Under the Treaty of Versailles, the Germans were pushed out. They were not allowed any territory west of the Rhine or to have any troops within 50km east of the Rhine. Thus they lost Alsace and Lorraine, and also the Saar. But the Saar was separated from the Rhine province in 1920, and put under League of Nations control for 15 years when a referendum would determine its future.

At the same time the largely German areas of Eupen and Malmedy were transferred to Belgium, and remain a German-speaking area of Belgium today.

The Germans were not managing to pay the reparations that were due under the Versailles Treaty, and using this justification, the French occupied the Rhineland (mainly the Ruhr Valley 1923-25). In 1936 Hitler reoccupied the Rhineland.

Although Germany had a good claim to Alsace-Lorraine (west of the Rhine; French since 1919; largely German-speaking), Hitler did not attempt to claim it before the war. During the war France, including Alsace Lorraine, was occupied by Germany.

We can see that, long before the outbreak of WW2, and the partition of Czechoslovakia, the provisions of the Treaty of Versailles were falling apart, and not through invasion by Germany. The provisions of the Treaty regarding disarmament were disregarded by all.

Different countries felt free to agree whatever they wished, regardless of Versailles. Various bilateral treaties were agreed that departed from Versailles. We can also see that Poland was not a helpless, innocent virgin to which the West should give priority protection.

Some writers have argued that the severity of the Treaty has been exaggerated. But most seem to be clear about its humiliating terms for Germany. Hitler certainly adopted that view. Politicians are generally willing to say whatever is necessary to gain, extend and retain power. The argument that the reparations were impossibly excessive, and that Germany had been totally humiliated by the Treaty, soon gained traction, with disastrous consequences.

In March 1935 Hitler announced the expansion of German armed forces to 600,000 – six times the number permitted by Versailles – and the development of an air force and a larger navy. The League of Nations condemned this, but did virtually nothing to stop it. In March 1936 Hitler occupied the demilitarised Rhineland.

In 1937 Germany and Italy became allies.

In March 1938 Hitler annexed Austria (the 'Anschluss'), having threatened invasion. Austria was German-speaking, and Hitler was widely welcomed. It was not generally seen as an 'invasion' and did not cause major international protest.

Next on the list was Czechoslovakia.

Czechoslovakia was created at the end of World War 1 when Austria-Hungary was dismembered. It was an ill-conceived non-country, as subsequent events demonstrate.

The Duke of Windsor said (of Czechoslovakia) in 1937:

It's a ridiculous country. It isn't a nation at all, but an invention of

Woodrow Wilson[9]. How could anyone go to war for a country like that?[10]

In a broadcast on 27 Sept 1938 Chamberlain referred to the Czechoslovakia dispute as:

A quarrel between people in a far-away country of whom we know nothing.

(In 1993 Czechoslovakia, a 'country' that should never have existed, was divided into two countries: Slovakia and the Czech Republic.)

There were no traditional borders and its population was very mixed. There were about 7,000,000 Czechs, 3,500,000 Germans, 2,000,000 Slovaks, 700,000 Hungarians, and 450,000 Ruthenians. It included the overwhelmingly German Sudetenland (one third of the whole country). More than 23% of Czechoslovakia's total population was German speaking. Some parts of Czechoslovakia were overwhelmingly Hungarian.

The Sudeten Germans demanded autonomy, and in 1935 the Sudetan German Party obtained over two thirds of the vote in that area, and, probably with German support, pushed for greater autonomy – more than the Czech government was willing to allow. Arguing for their right to self-determination, Hitler threatened to invade Sudetenland (which was largely surrounded by Germany).

In 1938 the British Prime Minister, Chamberlain, sought peace and to diffuse the crisis. He had meetings with Hitler in September 1938, and agreed that Sudetenland should become part of Germany. The

---

9   Woodrow Wilson (1856-1924), President of America 1913-1921; famous for his *fourteen points* in forming the Treaty of Versailles, and establishing the League of Nations. He then had a severe stroke and was unable to obtain Senate approval for these achievements

10   Higham, p 280

French similarly agreed, and although the Czech government was excluded from the discussions, their government reluctantly agreed to abide by the conclusions.

When Chamberlain returned to London (Heston Aerodrome, near Heathrow), he was met by large, enthusiastic crowds. He said that the Anglo-German Naval Agreement was 'symbolic of the desire of our two peoples never to go to war with one another again'. He said he brought 'peace with honour' and 'peace for our time'. He was met at Heston by the Lord Chamberlain, bearing a letter from King George VI assuring him of the Empire's lasting gratitude and urging him to come straight to Buckingham Palace. His journey was slowed by the large crowds, but he appeared on the balcony with the King and Queen. Duff Cooper resigned as First Lord of the Admiralty, but the Munich Agreement was very widely welcomed, by the crowds, by most newspapers, and Parliament. No-one in the Conservative Party voted against it, but there were 20 or so abstentions, including Winston Churchill, Duff Cooper[11], Anthony Eden[12] and Harold Macmillan[13].

Butler[14] said:

---

11   Duff Cooper (1890-1954); labelled by German propaganda as one of the three most dangerous Conservative warmongers

12   Anthony Eden (1897-1977); Foreign Secretary 1935-8, 1940-45 and 1951-55; Prime Minister 1955-57

13   Harold Macmillan (1894-1986); Junior Minister 1940-45; Senior Minister 1951-57; Prime Minister 1957-63

14   'RAB'Butler (1902-1982), Under Secretary of State for Foreign Affairs 1938-40 representing Lord Halifax in the House of Commons. Subsequently in charge of Education. After the war he served in most major government posts, and frequently deputised for Churchill. He never became Prime Minister, perhaps because he was seen as favouring 'Appeasement'

I can see no alternative to the policy upon which the Prime Minister has so courageously set himself and more importantly ***War settles nothing***[15].

Perhaps he held the view that generally, and particularly in the light of WW1, wars do more harm than good.

The welcome for Chamberlain's 'Peace' did not last long.

Churchill was already manoeuvring to try to take advantage of the situation. He opened secret negotiations with the Labour Party using Harold Macmillan as his intermediary with Hugh Dalton. With the unpleasing prospect of another 'Coupon' Election on the pattern of 1918, he wanted to find a common platform with Labour.[16]

Befriending the Labour Party was key to his becoming Prime Minister on 10 May 1940.

Britain declared war on Germany on September 3, 1939. Two days previously Hitler had invaded Poland, and Britain needed to act because of the 'Polish Guarantee'. At 9am on the 3rd, an ultimatum was presented at the German Foreign Office which expired two hours later. When the ultimatum expired, Chamberlain declared that Britain was at war with Germany.

---

15   RAB's apparent pacifist sympathies did not endear him to Tory warmongers, and probably prevented him from becoming Tory Party Leader in the years after the War.

16   Charmley, p 355

Arms Race 1932-39

Armaments	Britain	France	Russia	Germany
Military Aircraft				
1932	445	400	2,595	36
1939	7,940	3,163	10,382	8,295
Major Warships				
1932	284	175	89	26
1939	290	161	101	88
Army				
1932	192,000	350,000	562,000	100,000
1939	237,000	500,000	1,900,000	730,000
Military Expenditure				
1932	£107 m	13.8bn fr	1.4 bn rbls	RM 0.61bn
1939	£397.4 m	28.1bn fr	27 m rbls	RM 17.24bn

Germany started the 1930s well behind Britain or France. The combination of Britain and France left Germany hopelessly out-numbered. This was because of the restrictions placed on Germany by the Treaty of Versailles.

After Hitler came to power there was a massive increase in the number of military aircraft. The arms race was very real.

There were some modest increases in the number of major warships, but a much bigger proportionate increase in Germany. However, Germany's fleet remained small compared with Britain or France. This suggests that Germany was more interested in fighting on land than across the seas; and that a German invasion of Britain was not a priority.

Britain and France's armies increased relatively modestly. But there were massive increases in Russia and Germany, as if preparing for the battles to come. Germany's army had been very small, but Hitler steadily increased it to rival Britain and France combined. However, the Russians clearly outnumbered the German army.

In total military expenditure there were massive increases all round. It was a serious arms race.

After WW1 there was pressure for limited disarmament. One of Wilson's 'fourteen points', which were agreed in 1918, was 'adequate guarantees given and taken that national armaments will be reduced to the lowest point consistent with domestic safety'. German arms were immediately reduced to that level, but others did not follow. Not unnaturally, Germany felt threatened by her neighbours who maintained significantly (and increasingly) higher levels of troops and forces and armaments than were permitted to Germany.

British disarmament, or rather reductions in armaments, was not initiated as an example to others.[17]

The international disarmament conference in 1932 failed. Britain insisted on maintaining a substantial air force and navy. France and Germany distrusted each other. France would not accept equality with Germany. Britain would not guarantee France against German bad faith. In October 1933 Germany withdrew from the disarmament conference, and from the League of Nations. It was the year in which Hitler had become Chancellor. He soon realised that other countries' promises of disarmament had come to nothing. Germany's WW1 enemies would not honour their promises – which were perhaps no more than

---

17   A J P Taylor, *Oxford History*, p 227

A pious declaration that this was a preliminary to general disarmament[18].

If the Allies could ignore the terms of WW1 settlements, so could the Germans. Post WW2 'history' has emphasised that Hitler's word could not be trusted. Similarly, Britain's promises to disarm, or to defend Poland, were worthless.

Much of the above may over-emphasise the importance of events and of particular persons. Britain, France and Germany were three powers vying to be 'top dog'. Britain wanted to rule the waves (sea and sky); France wanted to be secure (from Germany). As each country established more armaments, supposedly to defend against Germany, so Germany felt increasingly threatened, and needed to re-arm. An arms race is a powerful precursor to war.

Meanwhile, the politicians were like flotsam and jetsam amidst uncontrollable waves, struggling to stay on top, each vying for position, reputation and power.

18　A J P Taylor, *Oxford History*, p 135

Chapter 3
Poland

Poland was central to the outbreak of WW2 which led from the ill-judged and reckless guarantee given to Poland by Chamberlain (similar to the one already given by France) in 1939.

Although Poland can trace its history for more than a thousand years, much of the time it had been divided between its neighbours, with uncertain frontiers. In 1807 the French Napoleon I created the temporary satellite state, the Duchy of Warsaw; but it was divided amongst the anti-Napoleon allies, Russia, the Austrian Empire and the German Confederation at the Congress of Vienna in 1815. Poland did not exist again as an independent country until it was re-established at the Treaty of Versailles in 1919. It was recognised that parts of 'Poland' were mainly German-speaking, and East Prussia, part of Germany, continued to exist in the north-east of 'Poland', separated from the rest of Germany by the 'Polish Corridor' which terminated in the north with the important, but disputed (about 95 % German) port of Danzig, which was established as a 'Free City'.

Most of what is now regarded as northern Poland, including West Prussia and East Prussia, and the whole Baltic coast as far east as (but not including) Lithuania was part of the German Empire from 1871-1914. Perhaps it should not have been, as large minorities of the population were Poles, not Germans, and in some areas Polish speakers were the majority. At the end of World War 1, the Second Polish Republic was granted much of what is now northern Poland, parts of which had a German-speaking majority. Hitler could not and did not argue that the whole of Poland should be part of Germany, although it is understandable that he would want to include most of what was regarded as part of Germany before WW1. He signed a non-aggression pact with Russia, whereby they could divide Poland between them. The German invasion of Poland began on September 1, 1939; the Russians invaded 16 days later. Britain declared war on Germany on September 3, 1939, as did France, Australia and New Zealand, followed by South Africa and Canada a few days later. Thus Poland was divided between Russia and Germany, with smaller areas taken by Lithuania and Slovakia, and WW2 had begun.

Poland was defeated more quickly than Britain and France (and Poland) had expected – too quickly for them to be able to offer much help – whether or not they intended to.

Following the Polish-Soviet War (1920), the Peace of Riga 1921 had given Western Ukraine to Poland. Autonomy had been promised, but was not delivered, Polish nationalist policies were enforced, and a powerful, right wing, underground (and later terrorist) Ukrainian nationalist movement soon developed. This was caused by, and led to, Polish persecution of Ukrainians.

The newly independent Poland made a very bad start, at least in the eyes of western democracies. The Jews were subject to a continuous hail of verbal attacks, and widespread violence, much of it exceedingly cruel and humiliating. A 1927 Law required that all artisans be technically competent not just in their work, but also in the Polish language. Another 1927 Law placed limits on the kosher slaughtering of animals. Anti-Semitic parties grew up in the late 1930s. In the late 1930s a whole series of laws and requirements were introduced that seemed to be targeted at Jewish businesses, and at Jews being professionals. For example, all shop signs had to display the names of the owners; the Polish Medical Association excluded Jews from the medical profession in 1937; in 1938 restrictions were placed on the ability of Jewish lawyers to practise law; in that same year the Bank Polski adopted discriminatory measures and the General Assembly of Journalists excluded Jews. Poland had a very large number of Jews, and it became increasingly evident that they were not welcome. The Polish Government tried, and failed, to get agreement to send many to (French) Madagascar. Even the Catholic Church seemed to be anti-Semitic (although condemning the assaulting of Jews or destroying their premises). Cardinal Hlond said:

It is an actual fact that Jews fight against the Catholic Church, they are freethinkers and constitute the vanguard of atheism, bolshevism and revolution ... in schools the Jewish youth is having an evil influence. One does well to avoid Jewish shops and Jewish stalls in the market...One should protect oneself against the influence of Jewish morals.

Indeed anti-Semitism in Poland was so deep-rooted that Jews did not feel safe living there even after the war, and after Hitler had killed himself. Hundreds were murdered between 1945 and 1947. Thousands emigrated. Perpetrators often went unpunished. Many Poles believed ridiculous old blood libel tales that Jews killed Christian children for their blood.

If WW2 was to defeat anti-Semitism, a common post-war argument, it was remarkably unsuccessful. Britain's participation in the war, on the side of Poland, was more about winning the war at all costs than it was about helping the Jews.

Poland needed to learn how to be a country again. The Polish constitution (1919) had established the country as a Parliamentary Democracy: the President had limited powers. He was elected by the Parliament, and he appointed the Government. He could dissolve the Lower House, and call elections, only with the consent of the Upper House; and he could issue decrees only if agreed by the Prime Minister and another relevant minister. There were many different parties, often representing ethnic minorities (Germans, Jews, Ukrainians, Belarusian), and frequently changing governments which became unpopular, with accusations of corruption, and coup attempts.

Two important problems were:

i. Germany wanted to control the Free City of Danzig (overwhelmingly German, but surrounded by Poland and subject to much Polish control); and
ii. Germany could not access part of its country (East Prussia) by land, except by going through Polish territory. The Polish Corridor, between the two parts of Germany was about 32-112 km wide.

Germany wanted to build a road and a railway between East Prussia and the rest of Germany, crossing the Polish Corridor. Poland objected that the road and the railway would cut them off from the sea. But this would seem to be something that could have been negotiated, if there had been the will. Warsaw had easy sea access via the river Vistula. Moreover, it should not have been difficult to build railway and road bridges so that Poles would not be 'blocked' from the sea, and could easily cross the German routes.

But Poland did not trust Germany. Germany had ruled much of Poland for most of the previous century, and Germany had broken other agreements, such as the Munich Agreement on Czechoslovakia.

There was a sea ferry service between East Prussia and the rest of Germany; there were also sealed trains across the Corridor. But Germany had justified grievances. Germans in the Polish Corridor had been victimised and their lands confiscated. The discrimination suffered by Germans within western Poland may have been exaggerated for propaganda purposes. But it seems that the Polish language was enforced; and many Germans left. There were also problems with the sealed trains: many Germans feared over-officious Polish customs officers. There was a serious train accident (May 1925) in the Polish Corridor where someone had removed vital parts of the rail track, causing the deaths of 25 passengers. This was attributed to anti-German terrorism.

Poland felt under threat from Hitler. This

... had provoked discriminatory measures against [ethnic Germans] and some 70,000 fled to the Reich in late August [1939][19].

Marshal Pilsudski, wanting to heal the country's excessive divisions, took power in a military coup in 1926, then retained power in successive elections. He died shortly after the adoption of an authoritarian constitution in 1936. Until 1939 the country was said to be governed by 'Pilsudski's Colonels'.

As Hitler wanted to re-establish the German borders of 1914, and overturn the Treaty of Versailles, there was obviously going to be trouble in this area, and it was the immediate cause of the war in September 1939. But negotiations continued throughout July and August, and it seems that Britain was prepared to agree to most of what Hitler wanted[20] in an attempt to maintain peace. But Poland was intransigent, and would concede nothing, although Germany's claim to Danzig was perfectly reasonable, and the Polish Corridor

---

19   Beevor, p 18
20   For example, Sir Horace Wilson, a close friend and associate of Chamberlain, made clear that provided Hitler abandoned his aggressive stance towards Poland, London would be prepared to discuss the return of Danzig and the Polish corridor to Germany, along with former German colonies, economic concessions, and disarmament generally [Messerschmidt, M, *Foreign Policy and Preparation for war*, taken from *Germany and the Second World War* p706-7]. Comparable negotiations with Britain and Germany were conducted by Lord Kemsley and the Swedish businessmen Axel Wenner-Gren and Birger Dahlerus [Watt, D C, *How War Came* London, Heinemann, 1989, p 394-407]

could have been settled by plebiscite. Conventional wisdom says that German aggression was responsible for the outbreak of WW2. It could equally be argued that Polish intransigence was responsible.

Six months earlier (March 31, 1939) Britain (following France) had guaranteed Polish independence in the following terms:

'... in the event of any action which clearly threatened Polish independence, and which the Polish Government accordingly considered it vital to resist with their national forces, His Majesty's Government would feel themselves bound at once to lend the Polish Government all support in their power'.

It is worth repeating that the British Government would feel themselves **bound at once to lend the Polish Government all support in their power.**

It was rather less than a promise to go to war with Germany, although it has usually been interpreted as such. The British Government did not have it in their power to prevent the German (and Russian) conquest of Poland. The British army was too small, and too far away to do anything 'at once', or perhaps anything much at all.

Britain had promised 'all support within their power'. That could mean lending money, providing a home and support for a Polish Government in exile, limited military support and advice, even some aircraft. Moral support would have been better than war. Attempts to reach an international negotiated settlement would have been the moral choice, the preference of statesmen. It was not the choice of warmongers who preferred a war with Germany.

Of course it is argued that Hitler was determined to invade Poland, and no negotiation would have stopped him. By September 1st, or a few days earlier, that was probably true. But statesmen should have tackled the problem earlier, and with urgency, before it was too late.

Many would argue that an international alliance plus moral pressure and concessions (over Danzig and the Polish Corridor) would not have been enough to stop the German invasion. But that was Britain's policy in the summer of 1939. It was not effective because Britain and France were too weak – Hitler was not deterred by their combined 'might'. He was an opportunist; and Britain did not pursue potentially effective policies with enough urgency and vigour before it was too late.

A more powerful alliance could have been effective, perhaps including Belgium, the Netherlands, Denmark, Norway, and some other countries subsequently over-run by Germany. It was, indeed, a more powerful alliance that did eventually defeat Hitler. The British Government knew, before declaring war, that they did not have a sufficiently powerful alliance to stop Hitler. They had tried to form an alliance with Russia to protect Poland, but the Poles would not wear it. The British Government knew that they were dependent on the Americans to continue with the war. They hardly bothered with smaller countries. In the end the Allies depended on Russia to defeat Hitler. A dreadful war could have been avoided if Britain had first concentrated on building the alliances that they knew to be essential to stop Hitler from invading Poland.

Chamberlain issued the 'guarantee'. This was particularly stupid,

'the maddest single action this country has ever taken'. It was 'foolish, futile and provocative ...[and] ill considered[21]

This was because:

---

21   Quoted in Buchanan, p 255-6

1. **It was unrealistic and impractical.** Britain simply did not have sufficient forces to be able to honour the Guarantee and to defend Poland against Germany. Britain's forces were not ready for a quick German strike; and Poland was too far away – on the other side of Germany – for there to be any practical prospect of getting there. Lloyd George said [of Chamberlain]

   ... he rushed into the first rash and silly enterprise that entered his uninformed mind ... sheer madness.[22]

2. **It was a bluff.** It was hoped that Hitler would be scared of a combined threat from Britain and France. But he was not. He knew it was a bluff of no practical significance. Britain's credibility was undermined.

   When Lloyd George was told by Chamberlain that the pact would deter Hitler, he burst out laughing, and said that if the British Army General Staff had approved it, they ought to be confined to a lunatic asylum. [23]

3. **It was a lie** if it was intended that Poland should have believed that they would receive any military help from Britain.

4. **It was dishonourable** to promise support, and then not deliver it.

5. **It provoked Hitler.** Prior to the guarantee he was negotiating with the Poles, but once the Poles had their 'guarantee' they no longer thought that they needed to negotiate. Hitler's relatively modest requests (most of which were agreeable to the British Government) could not be met by negotiation. He was provoked

---

22   Buchanan, p 266

23   Peter Rowland, *David Lloyd George,* Macmillan p 757

into war.

6. **It also provoked Poland** to be more intransigent; they no longer needed to make concessions – they had the British (and French) guarantee. According to Ponting,

The guarantee to Poland was hurriedly put together in the face of military advice not to go ahead. The cabinet hoped the guarantee would place them in a position to put pressure on the Poles to reach a settlement[24].

In fact it did just the opposite.

Two days before Hitler invaded Poland, further negotiations took place between Britain and Poland. According to the American Ambassador, Chamberlain was more worried about getting the Poles to be reasonable than the Germans.

7. **It established British (theoretical) presence in Eastern Europe.** By establishing Britain's [theoretical] presence in eastern Europe, according to Butler

It relieved Russia of any real anxiety about Germany's designs on her own frontier ... It thus led Russia to going in with Germany[25].

He is thus arguing that the Anglo-French Polish guarantee reduced Russia's fear of Germany and led to the two countries agreeing to divide Poland between them.

8. **It gave to Poland the decision whether Britain should go to war.** The guarantee stated that any action which *the*

---

24   Ponting, *1940 Myth and Reality*, p37-9
25   Howard, *Butler, Life, p 85*

Polish government considered it vital to resist with their national forces would bring about British help. It was what the Polish government considered vital that was the determinant of whether Britain should go to war. Britain seemed to have no say in the matter.

It placed Britain's destiny in the hands of Polish rulers, men of unstable and dubious judgment. [26]

Never before in our history have we left in the hands of one of the smaller powers the decision whether or not Britain goes to war. [27]

... the most reckless undertaking ever given by a British government. It placed the decision on peace or war in Europe in the hands of a reckless intransigent, swashbuckling military dictatorship. [28]

9. **It was misleading.** It was often interpreted as guaranteeing Poland's borders, but the wording was about Poland's independence, not about its borders. Britain was happy to negotiate with Hitler about the Polish Corridor, and Danzig. The Poles had no guarantee that they could retain these (although they behaved as if they had).

Moreover it is widely assumed that the guarantee to the Poles was to apply in the event of a German invasion of Poland. But it applied equally to any European power which invaded Poland.

If the guarantee meant that Britain had to declare war on Germany when Germany invaded Poland, then it also meant that Britain had to declare war on Russia 16 days later, when Russia

---

26 Buchanan, p 256
27 Duff Cooper, *Diaries*, p 407
28 Denman, R, *Missed Chances*, Cassell, 1997, p 121

invaded Poland. But it seemed that Britain wanted a war with Germany, not with Russia, and used the German invasion as an excuse or justification for going to war (with Germany).

Hitler is often seen as a wicked butcher, with his secret police, murders and death camps – most of it occurring after war was declared. But Stalin was at least as bad before war was declared.

There is no case for Britain declaring war on Germany that did not apply equally to declaring war on Russia. Yet Russia became Britain's ally.

10. **It was unnecessary and unprecedented** to issue such guarantees, and Britain had no important national interests in that area. According to Austin Chamberlain, the Polish Corridor was something

> ... *for which no British Government ever will and ever can risk the bones of a British grenadier.* [29]

11. **It was too personal.** Chamberlain was clearly a man of peace, but he was also personally offended that Hitler should go against his word on Czechoslovakia, and it was partly a fit of pique that led him to advocate this disastrous guarantee. He said

> *Hitler let me down shamefully ... he seems to be a revengeful little thing.*[30]

---

29 Letter to Sir Eyre Crowe, Feb 16 1925. This was Austin Chamberlain, not the Neville Chamberlain (his half-brother) who was Prime Minister later. Unless otherwise specified, all other references to Chamberlain are to Neville Chamberlain

30 Self, p 351

Buchanan's view is that

Deceived and betrayed by Hitler, his Munich pact made a mockery, Chamberlain appears to have acted out of shame and humiliation at having been played for a fool, out of fear of Tory backbenchers who had turned against Munich in disgust, and out of panic that Germany was out to dominate the world.[31]

12. **It was a jump into the unknown.** Chamberlain, who was fond of using fox-hunting metaphors, said that one should not jump into a field until one can see a way of jumping out:

...occasionally it is necessary to do so. In the case of the Polish guarantee a jump from a dangerous main road had suddenly to be made over a high hedge in cold blood. [32]

This is significant because it shows:

a. He did not know what the consequences would be, and he could not see how to get out of it – presumably he was very aware that it could well lead to war; and

b. He thought it had to be done 'suddenly' – there appeared to be no carefully considered planning or diplomacy. Self[33] reckoned he had been stampeded into action.

13. **It was issued by Chamberlain personally,** without consulting the Dominions (which came to Britain's help when the consequent war was declared), although he and Halifax had rushed it through the British Cabinet acting on

---

31   Buchanan, p 266
32   Howard, p 83
33   Self, p 367

... hot-headed impulse, instead of with the cool-headed judgment that was once characteristic of British statesmanship. [34]

14. **It was based on an underestimate of German strength** and of Hitler's position. According to Self, in the winter 1938-9, Chamberlain was in receipt of a steady flow of (inaccurate and misleading) secret intelligence from the German conservative 'resistance' to Hitler, suggesting that he was barely sane, consumed by intense hatred of this country (UK) and capable of ordering an immediate attack on any European country and having his command instantly obeyed. Some in Britain seemed to believe that they could defeat Hitler. They could not (without substantial help from major powers). Throughout, Britain and France seem to have had an exaggerated idea of their own power and importance.

15. **A Four Power Guarantee was needed** (Britain, France, Russia and Poland) to be effective, but the Poles did not want the Russians involved. (They were too fearful of what Russian 'help' and 'troops' would lead to.) Hitler would have preferred an alliance with Britain and with Poland.

Although Churchill welcomed the government's attempts to stand up to Hitler, he said at the time that none of these

...sets of assurances had any military value except within the framework of a general agreement with Russia. [35]

16. **Poland was not a defenceless innocent victim** or an ideal ally. They had a much larger army than Britain (although only about half were mobilised, in line with British advice to avoid

---

34   Several sources quoted in Buchanan, p 260
35   Churchill in Hansard, 5th series, Vol 347, Cols 1840-9

provoking war). Polish forces had the advantage of being in Poland. British forces were far away, either in Britain, or scattered through the empire.

Britain had a long tradition of Parliamentary democracy (as did its allies, France and, later, America; though not, of course, Russia). Poland's experiment with democracy did not last long and it was under an authoritarian military government. It was

... a regime no less authoritarian, nationalistic, totalitarian and racially intolerant than Germany ... in the hands of unstable and irresponsible leaders

... a regime that was every bit as undemocratic and anti-Semitic as that of Germany

Furthermore

Englishmen of all classes and of all parties were offended by the Nazi treatment of the Jews... .Jews were treated as badly in other countries, and often worse – in Poland for example. [36]

Poland was not shy of grabbing more territory where it could. Vilnius, the historic capital of independent Lithuania, was seized by Poland in 1920, and retained until WW2. The two countries remained on bad terms. In 1921, following the Polish-Soviet War, it obtained Western Ukraine. In 1938, following Hitler's invasion of Czechoslovakia, it obtained the Zaolzie part of that country.

One third of the population of Poland comprised various minorities, many of whom, following extreme Polonization of the areas they occupied, felt persecuted. Poland did not treat its

---

36   A J P Taylor, *Oxford*, p 419

minorities well, and disregarded its international obligations to do so.

Germany was Britain's enemy, supposedly because it was a non-democratic ruthless dictatorship, successfully grabbing other countries' territory, disregarding international obligations and treating its main minority population (Jews) badly. Poland (and Russia) were rather similar, but they were Britain's allies!

At first, Churchill supported the guarantee; he could hardly do otherwise in view of his consistent advocacy of standing up to Hitler, and if he wanted to be a member of Chamberlain's government. But he was soon to have doubts. A few years later he was to refer to Poland

... which with hyena appetite had only six months before joined in the pillage and destruction of the Czechoslovak state ... Moreover, how could we protect Poland and make good our guarantee? ... Here was a decision taken at the worst possible moment and on the least satisfactory ground, which must surely lead to the slaughter of tens of millions of people. [37]

The guarantee to Poland should never have been given. Britain was not in a position to defend Poland, and the Polish leaders did not realise that the British were not ready for war – they needed time to prepare.

In Britain, the mood in favour of Appeasement and the Munich Agreement did not last long.

In March 1939 the Germans invaded the remainder of Czechoslovakia, contravening Hitler's agreement with Chamberlain. He may have done it because of its strategic importance, or it may have been

---

37   Churchill, *Gathering Storm*, p 247

simple militaristic aggression; and it may be because he had no respect for Czechoslovakia as a country: it was falling apart anyway (and Hitler was largely responsible for its dismemberment). By early 1939, Poland and Hungary had each helped themselves to outlying parts of Czechoslovakia. The leader of Slovakia (the eastern part of the country) and his country had been bullied and threatened by Hitler, and had declared independence. Hitler established a 'protectorate' of what remained of Czechoslovakia (Bohemia and Moravia), after comparable bullying, followed by invasion. Hitler stated that 'Czechoslovakia showed its inherent inability to survive and has now therefore fallen victim to actual dissolution'. Hitler was steadily undoing the provisions of the Treaty of Versailles. Poland took several areas: Zaolzie, then northern Spisz, northern Orawa and some other smaller border areas. Polish was introduced as the only official language. It was as if Poland were collaborating with the Nazis in the dismemberment of Czechoslovakia. Indeed, Hitler was pleased that Poland was first to take over (small) parts of Czechoslovakia[38]. He took over most of the rest five months[39] later. Given that Poland and Hungary took part in the dismemberment of Czechoslovakia, Germany was not isolated as the guilty party.

But Hitler was mainly responsible for the dismemberment of Czechoslovakia – which was perhaps an innocent virgin. When it came to Poland, Britain and France (thought they) were ready for Hitler.

The Domino Theory

The words became popular in relation to Communism in the 1950s, but seem to have been applied to Hitler. If a wicked dictator or regime successfully invaded Area A, and then Area B, inevitably Areas C, D,

38 Early October 1938
39 March 16, 1939

WWII WAS BRITAIN RIGHT TO FIGHT?

and E would fall like a row of dominoes, and then the UK and then the world. It is an effective argument in favour of war, however little truth it contains. Wicked dictators invariably over-reach themselves, and whatever support they have mustered at home eventually weakens and fades.

Hitler had got away with annexing / invading Austria and most of Czechoslovakia. Now he was grabbing Poland, and, the warmongers would say, must not be allowed to get away with it; next would be Greece, Romania, Norway, Sweden, Denmark and Britain and the world. This domino theory was used to explain the need for extensive 'defensive' invasions. Within a year of the invasion of Poland, Lithuania and Slovakia helped themselves to small parts of Poland, Russia established their troops in Latvia, Lithuania and Estonia, invaded Finland and took parts of Romania (Besserabia, Herza and Northern Bukovina), and Britain invaded Iceland and the Faroes and planned to invade Greenland[40].There were no saints in this game of dominoes.

All-out war against Germany became advocated as the only solution, but was it?

The West felt that they had to make a stand against German expansion, and so the Polish guarantee was given. But, in practice, it was little more than an empty promise – much like the Munich Agreement. Britain was no more 'honourable' to Poland than Germany was to Czechoslovakia.

What If …?

The question is often asked "What would have happened if 'we' had not gone to war?". History is full of 'What Ifs'. The only certainty is

---

40   But America took over

that the War happened, and it was disastrous for Britain and many others. It did lead to Hitler's suicide, and the near destruction of Nazism. If 'we' had not gone to war Hitler would have invaded Poland and Russia, just as he did anyway. He would probably not have felt it necessary to defend his western front by invading France, Belgium, Luxembourg, the Netherlands, Denmark and Norway. There would still have been war between Russia and Germany, and we do not know which one would have defeated the other, or if it would have been long term stalemate. We do know that Eastern Europe would have been dominated by a wicked dictator, but we do not know whether it would have been Hitler or Stalin. We also know that the consequences of wars are unpredictable, and that there is no way of knowing if a war will do any good. A major war certainly does enormous harm.

Many people still glorify Britain's role in WW2 – Britain's finest hour. Britain sacrificed enormously, much more than could be afforded, supposedly in a great moral crusade. But was it worth it? Poland is the key that unlocks the moral question in two ways:

1. Germany was an immoral, totalitarian, military dictatorship; it was heavily anti-Semitic; it acted contrary to the Treaty of Versailles; it invaded other countries and successfully expanded its territory; it could not be trusted. This was all so immoral, that a war against Germany was justified. Or so the story goes. But all of these accusations could equally be made against Poland. And Poland may have been even worse in its treatment of foreign nationals. Yet Poland was Britain's ally in the war against Germany. The same arguments can be used about Russia. Britain's choice of friends and enemies was inconsistent, even bizarre.

2. Britain did not honour the Polish guarantee, and did nothing to help Poland. This story demolishes Britain's claim to the moral high ground.

Moreover, Britain's failure to (even partially) disarm after WW1 made it clear that Britain's promises could not be trusted any more than those of Hitler.

It could be argued that it was all worth it to stop Hitler's killing spree. But it did not. It may even have provoked Hitler to kill more Jews; it certainly did not stop him. And the war was certainly responsible for killing more people than died in the German concentration camps.

Chapter 4
Churchill's career

Winston Churchill was born in Blenheim Palace in 1874. Lord Randolph Churchill was his English aristocratic father; his mother was an American, Jennie Jerome. Initially he was brought up in Ireland, but went to fee-paying private schools in the south-east of England. He was not a good student, and bothered little with subjects that did not interest him; he did not like mathematics. In 1893 he left Harrow School to join the Royal Military College, Sandhurst, where he succeeded in gaining entrance at the third attempt. He became a Second Lieutenant in 1895, but the pay was not sufficient to maintain his lifestyle. He also became a war correspondent for various newspapers, and wrote books which increased his income considerably; he also often presented himself in a favourable light, and began to develop a reputation for himself.

But he was no mere writer. He saw plenty of action in Cuba, India, the Sudan and South Africa, and was often in real danger. He was engaged in politics in England and was a Conservative MP from 1900. In 1915 he also joined the British Army on the Western Front in World War 1[41], partly to restore his reputation, but there were real dangers too; sometimes he seemed to court danger – or so his own accounts suggest, and he was not afraid of action. But he did not get the promotions that he thought he deserved.

It seemed that Churchill enjoyed the excitement and glory of war; of being recognised as a brave fighter; the exhilaration of living in the open and the thrilling moments of keenest action. He loved the camaraderie and discipline of the army and said:

---

41   He stuck it for only five months (it was five and a half, but that included three weeks back in England)

It is a jolly life with nice people, and one doesn't mind the wet and cold and general discomfort[42].

Asquith's wife said of him:

Winston is longing to be in the trenches – dreaming war, big, buoyant, happy even. He is a born soldier[43] .

Churchill even blurted out that he found war 'delicious' – instantly pleading for her not to repeat the remark – and was heard to say that peace was the last thing we should pray for.[44]

Seldom has there been a statesman as good at glorifying war, as indecently eager to wage war, as Winston Churchill. All his works demonstrate his love of war, glamorise its glories, and minimise its horrors[45].

Whilst in the trenches he wrote:

'Amid these surroundings, aided by wet and cold, and every minor discomfort, I have found happiness and content such as I have not known for many months and slightly later *They all say I look five years younger: and certainly I have never been better in health and spirits [46].'* Churchill's patriotism and courage, highlighted by newspaper reports, some of which he wrote himself, enhanced his reputation and fame.

As Conservative MP for Oldham he opposed the government's military expenditure, and opposed the introduction of extensive

---

42   Quoted in Jacob Bannister, *Churchill*
43   Quoted in Johnson, p 169
44   Quoted in Johnson, p 169
45   Peregrine Worsthorne, former editor of *Sunday Telegraph*; quoted in Johnson, p 168
46   Roy Jenkins, *Churchill*, p 292-3

tariffs. He was a free-trader. He was never a proper Conservative, and in 1903, he said:

I hate the Tory Party, their men, their words, and their methods[47].

His constituency in Oldham de-selected him, and in 1904 he crossed the floor of the House and sat as a Liberal Member. A Liberal government took over in 1906, and he was elected as Liberal MP for Manchester North West, 1906-8, and became Under-Secretary of State for the Colonies, dealing mainly with South Africa. In 1908 he was appointed to the Cabinet as Secretary to the Board of Trade; at that time it was necessary for him to be re-elected. He won a by-election in Dundee as a Liberal in 1908.

The various causes with which he was associated read like a strange mixture today: he supported a range of Liberal reforms (1909-11), including the introduction of Labour Exchanges to help the unemployed to find work, the first unemployment pensions legislation, the first minimum wages legislation; he supported (unsuccessfully) eugenics and the sterilisation of the feeble minded; (unlike his views in the 1930s) he supported Lloyd George (Chancellor of the Exchequer) in opposing the First Lord of the Admiralty's proposals for substantial expenditure on warships. He supported the 'People's Budget' (1909-10), and was promoted to Home Secretary in 1910.

He appeared (perhaps unfairly) to be more reactionary in relation to the Suffragettes, the Rhondda Valley coal miners, and the Siege of Sidney Street.

Personal ambition rather than political conviction was still his main motivation, Lloyd George said of him. *He is an artist and will provide what is suitable for his audience.* He said of himself, *If I hadn't [left the*

---

47   John Charmley, p 31

Tory Party] I should now be its leader.[48]

He then served as First Lord of the Admiralty (1911-15) until after the Dardanelles Disaster. He started successfully, dynamically, and as a moderniser, encouraging the development of the tank, the conversion of ships from coal to oil, and the use of aircraft. But the disaster of the Gallipoli landings at the Dardanelles, for which he, perhaps unfairly, took much of the blame led to his downfall. The *Daily Mail*, on October 31 said, in relation to Churchill and the Dardanelles, that no politicians should be allowed to interfere with the relentless plans of Haig, and the Chief of the Imperial General Staff, Robertson. Above all he was a 'megalomaniac politician' who in the Dardanelles had 'risked the fate of our Army in France and sacrificed thousands of lives to no purpose'. The new coalition government, formed in 1915, demanded his demotion, after which he resigned from the Government, and then re-joined the army to fight in World War 1, whilst continuing as an MP.

He then said he was

Finished in respect of all I care for – the waging of war, the defeat of the Germans.[49]

Viscount Cecil[50] considered that Churchill was out of tune with the whole idea represented by the League of Nations; war was the only thing that interested him in politics. Cecil continued:

---

48   Ponting, *Churchill,* p 96-7
49   Jenkins, p 277
50   Lord Robert Cecil (1864-1958), later viscount Cecil of Chelwood; Lord Privy Seal (1923-4), Chancellor of the Duchy of Lancaster (1924-7) under Baldwin. Influential in forming League of Nations. Nobel Peace Prize 1937

I don't believe Winston takes any interest in public affairs unless they involve the possibility of bloodshed. Preferably he likes to kill foreigners, but he might be satisfied with a few native communists.[51]

His participation in World War 1 was successful and brave, though brief, and he recognised the danger of being killed. In a letter to his wife he said that his intention was to rehabilitate his reputation.

He remained an MP, and in little more than a year, he indicated that he wished to return to Parliament, and to speak. Lloyd George (soon to be Prime Minister)'s reply included the words

You will one day discover that the state of mind revealed in [your] letter is the reason why you do not win trust even when you command admiration. In every line of it, national interests are overshadowed by your personal concern. [52]

He re-joined the Coalition Government as Minister of Munitions 1917-1919, and then in 1919 as Secretary of State for War, and Secretary of State for Air (1919-21). He then became Secretary of State for the Colonies (1921-22) – apparently staying nowhere long enough to become bored. Throughout this period, he continued as Liberal MP for Dundee (1908-22).

In 1922 the Conservatives withdrew from the Coalition, forcing a General Election. Churchill lost his seat in Dundee. In the 1923 General Election, he stood again for the Liberals (in Leicester), but lost. In January 1924, the first Labour (minority) Government took office. In March 1924 he sought re-election in the Westminster Abbey by-election as an (anti-Labour) 'Constitutionalist'. He failed, but was elected in Epping with the 'Constitutionalist' label (with Conservative

---

51   Charmley, *Churchill,* p 236
52   Churchill-Lloyd George Correspondence, March 1926

support) in 1924, where he served as a Conservative MP 1924-45 (and then in the revised constituency of Epping 1945-64). He had changed party, again.

There were General Elections in 1922, 1923 and 1924.

In November 1922, the Conservatives won a clear overall majority over the Labour Party and the two Liberal Parties (pro- and anti-coalition). The Bonar Law[53] Conservative Government was formed, taking over from the Lloyd George Coalition. He was prime minister for only 211 days, and was succeeded by Baldwin in 1923.

In December 1923, there was no overall majority; the Conservatives were the largest single party, but Labour and Liberal combined were substantially larger. A minority Labour Government took office the following month.

In October 1924, there was a substantial overall Conservative majority; the Liberals were much reduced. Ramsey MacDonald's Labour minority Government had been formed in January 1924 but served for less than a year. Baldwin returned as Prime Minister in November 1924, and Churchill was appointed Chancellor of the Exchequer.

As Chancellor of the Exchequer he has been most criticised for returning Britain to the Gold Standard which was seen as contributing to the Depression. At the time the decision was popular and assumed to be good economics. But it was opposed by John Maynard Keynes, Lord Beaverbrook and the Federation of British Industries and subsequently Churchill was to regard it as the greatest mistake of his life. He survived various reactionary stances (eg apparently

---

53   Andrew Bonar Law (1858-1923), Conservative Party Leader, and Prime Minister October 23rd 1922 – May 22nd 1923

advocating the use of guns against the miners in the General Strike in 1926, praising Mussolini, opposing Gandhi and his civil disobedience – Churchill wanted to retain British power in India). It is easy to find criticisms of any politicians; there are always issues that do not turn out as expected, and with the best will in the world, no politician can get everything right. However, the general impression that he created was more important.

Winston Churchill is accused of being a spoilt, bullying, double-crossing, self-centred bore, and a bit of an all-round brute[54].

Whilst he was Chancellor of the Exchequer there was serious discussion of the possibility of him becoming Prime Minister, but he had made too many enemies. Arguments over the issue of de-rating strengthened Chamberlain's doubts about Churchill's suitability for the Premiership.[55] Douglas Hogg (Attorney General, later Lord Hailsham), who was Chamberlain's favourite (to succeed Baldwin), said:

I don't want to see W Churchill Prime Minister.[56]

Shortly before the 1929 General Election there was speculation that the Liberals might hold the balance of power afterwards. Baldwin and Chamberlain were both determined that they would not serve with Lloyd George, in which case Baldwin thought the leadership would go to Churchill.[57]

The Conservative Government, including Churchill, lost office after the 1929 General Election, when the second Labour minority

---

54 Quoted in Johnson – who disagrees with this verdict
55 Charmley, p 232
56 Charmley, p 233
57 Charmley, p 236-7

Government was formed.

Churchill then spent ten years 'in the wilderness' until he was made First Lord of the Admiralty again at the start of World War 2. The idea of his becoming Prime Minister seemed to have passed, but probably not in his mind.

He did not build up an alliance of friends and colleagues during that period. Indeed, he seemed to court controversy, and succeeded in falling out with people. He soon became estranged from the Conservative leadership over its policies (particularly the introduction of tariffs, and Home Rule for India), and made friendships outside politics, some of which were seen as dubious. He distanced himself from Baldwin, and did not serve under him in the 1930s. In the early 1930s he appeared to be more against communism (and socialism) than against the Nazis (though he was critical of their anti-Semitism).

Churchill was 60 in 1934, and it seemed that his political career was over. After the 1935 General Election, which the Conservatives won handsomely, Beaverbrook commented to Churchill

Well you're finished now; with such a good majority, Baldwin will be able to do without you[58].

As events turned out, it was WW2 which saved, or created, his career and reputation. But he was not to know that in the 1930s, although he probably had the possibility in mind. But in 1936 an opportunity arose which might have rescued his failing career. As it turned out, his stand did him more harm than good. But it gave him what might have been his last chance to become Prime Minister.

King George V died in 1936. He had been determined not to have

---

58   Charmley, p 297

another war with Germany. In 1935 he said:

*I will not have another war. **I will not**. The last one was not of my doing and if there is another one and we are threatened with being brought into it, I will go to Trafalgar Square and wave a red flag myself sooner than allow this country to be brought in[59].*

At least he seemed more aware of the limitations of his power than his son Edward VIII who thought he could do much more than wave flags.

When King George V died[60], many in the political Establishment were unhappy with his populist successor, King Edward VIII[61]. In part it was due to his careless and cocky attitude; but there were more serious matters. He seemed to want to be a political force in his own right. On St David's Day 1936 he refused point-blank to show a radio speech to the Home Secretary in advance of the broadcast[62]. This was a clear breach of constitutional requirements as laid down by precedent, and it was potentially dangerous to have a loose cannon around. As it happens, the speech turned out to be mild and uncontroversial.

Edward VIII also wanted to give a speech in March 1936 supporting greater Indian self-determination[63]; the Home Secretary removed

---

59   Letter to Lloyd George following Mussolini's invasion of Abyssinia, May 1935
60   Or was murdered by his doctor who administered lethal drugs to a dying man so that his death would be in time to be reported in the next morning's *Times*, rather than being relegated to the evening papers
61   Edward, oldest son of George V, 1894-1972, older brother of King George VI (reigned 1936-1952); King Edward VIII Jan-Dec 1036; abdicated; married Wallis Simpson; they became Duke and Duchess of Windsor
62   Morton, p 102
63   Picknett, *Windsors,* p 105

that passage from the speech; Edward, unsuccessfully, resisted. The Government could not tolerate the King having his own policies.

In July he proposed calling a conference to try to resolve the situation in Ireland; to do so is not the role of a constitutional monarch.

There were also concerns about Edward VIII's slipshod way of dealing with Government paperwork, often leaving it around for days, for anyone to see, whilst it acquired stains from drinks that had been placed on it. It seemed that certain would-be state secrets known to Edward, were soon known to the German Ambassador in London (Ribbentrop), and then extensively circulated in Germany. Wallis Simpson was widely believed to be the source.

It seemed that Edward VIII was not happy with his role as a constitutional monarch; he wanted more power and influence. He is reported, when discussing the Prime Minister's attitude to Germany, as saying

Who is King here, Baldwin or I? I wish to talk to Hitler, and will do so, here or in Germany.[64]

He could even have become some sort of mild dictator who was anti-Russian, pro-German, and friends with the likes of Oswald Mosley.

It is clear that Prime Minister Baldwin wanted to get rid of him, and Edward's intention to marry the twice divorced American, Wallis Simpson, provided the ideal opportunity. Baldwin played the situation very astutely, so that most people saw only the unacceptability of divorce, rather than the political manoeuvrings behind the scenes.

But Edward VIII had his friends and supporters and was reasonably

---

64   Cadbury, p 61

popular in this country and in Germany, as well as being the (only) legitimate king. In November 1936 Edward VIII toured the South Wales Coalfields, an area severely affected by poverty and unemployment. He said 'something should be done', which may seem fairly vague and non-committal. But it made him more popular with working people and the unemployed, and unpopular with the government, who thought he should not interfere.

In 1936 Hitler was testing the Treaty of Versailles to see how far he could go without provoking war. Germany was forbidden from having troops in the Rhineland. Hitler called a meeting of the British, French, Belgian and Italian ambassadors and informed them that he had repudiated the treaty and ordered his troops to re-occupy the Rhineland. It was a gamble. Later it turned out that he had given orders to his troops to withdraw if they met any resistance. The breach of the Treaty was condemned, but Hitler got away with it, without war.

However, for a few days Hitler had been worried. He did not know what would happen. Speer records that Hitler was relieved to receive a message from London and told Speer:

At last. The King of England will not intervene. He is keeping his promise.[65]

It seemed that someone[66] had appealed to the King to use his influence to ensure that the British Government did not react to the re-occupation of the Rhineland. The King claimed to have sent for Baldwin and told him that if the Government decided on a military response he would abdicate. This is important, and even amazing, because it seems to show:

---

65 Albert Speer (1905-1991), Hitler's architect, then Minister of Armaments and War Production (1942-45); 'The Nazi who said sorry'
66 Von Hoesche. Full details are given in Picknett et al, *Windsors*

a. That the King was pro-German, and did not support war with Germany; and
b. He was determined to use whatever influence he could muster, including the threat of abdication, to try to ensure the success of his stance.

If he had abdicated at that juncture it would have split the nation, and probably caused the Government to fall – because of a policy disagreement with the King. As things turned out, they were eventually able to blame the abdication on Wallis Simpson and her divorces. But the nation was divided over the issue, and disagreements and rancour could have been much worse. As it was, two of the King's most powerful supporters were Churchill and Beaverbrook. Beaverbrook wanted the King to get Baldwin to 'advise' him to abdicate; the King could then reject that advice, and the Prime Minister would have to resign. The King could then choose his own Prime Minister: Winston Churchill.

Before making a move, Churchill took advice from Prof J H Morgan, a former adviser to the Indian Defence League, on the possibility of his forming a government. Morgan's view was that if the King insisted on marrying, and not abdicating, and if Baldwin then resigned, and Labour[67] refused to form an alternative government, the King could call upon Churchill to form a government[68].

A member of Baldwin's Cabinet[69], the Marquess of Zetland, wrote:

It seems that the King has been encouraged to believe that Winston Churchill would in these circumstances be prepared to form an alternative Government. If this were true there would be a grave risk of the country

---

67   Labour and the Liberals had already promised not to
68   Ponting, *Churchill,* p 383-4
69   Secretary of State for India

being divided into two camps – for and against the King.

The King was also supported by the Imperial Policy Group who considered Communism and the Soviet Union the greater threat, and would leave it to Germany and the Soviet Union to exhaust themselves fighting each other while Britain stayed out. At the time William Morrison (Minister of Agriculture) and Leslie Hore-Belisha (Transport Minister) feared a coup d'etat with Churchill being asked by the King to lead a Government of his 'friends', and then calling an election on the issue of the King's marriage.[70]

According to Higham,

meetings were held by the Imperial Policy Group [including] Kenneth de Courcy... interested and influential peers and MPs. The purpose was clear. The group wanted to force the King to call upon the government to resign or ... to pressure it into a position from which it would have to resign. The King would then send for Winston Churchill to form a new Government; the IPG was convinced that there were enough individuals in both the House of Commons and the House of Lords to achieve its purpose. De Courcy... believed that Churchill would have swept into power with an overwhelming majority.[71]

It is strange that Churchill, who was consistently keen on arming against, and even fighting Germany, should associate with the pro-German camp, and it is difficult to conclude anything other than he had an overwhelming desire to become Prime Minister.

One newspaper[72] declared that if the King married Mrs Simpson, Baldwin would be obliged to resign, and the King would need to

---

70   Charmley, p 317
71   Higham, *Mrs Simpson*, p181
72   *Daily Mirror* 4 Dec 1936

seek an alternative government to support him; that would require a general election; a King's party could split the country. The paper even contemplated a Royal Dictatorship where the King could attempt to govern without a parliament – given the European scene at the time, with dictatorships increasingly common, that would not have been completely impossible.

The idea that the King could choose to have his own man as Prime Minister seems very strange today. We assume that the King or Queen has to choose the leader of the largest party in Parliament. But as recently as 1963, in the days when the Conservatives did not elect their Leader, the Queen 'chose'[73] the leader, after taking appropriate soundings. And when Churchill eventually did become Prime Minister, he was not leader of the party[74]. It was not therefore necessary for the Prime Minister to be the Leader of the largest party, or of any party.

In 1940, King George VI 'chose' Churchill on the recommendation of Chamberlain, the Prime Minister.

Nine years earlier, King George V's choice of Prime Minister was more bizarre, personal and perhaps even unconstitutional. Although George V did not like the Labour Party, a Labour minority Government took office in 1929. George V liked the Labour leader, Ramsey MacDonald. In the middle of 1931 a financial and political crisis hit Britain and the King persuaded MacDonald to continue heading the Government as leader of a National Government. Labour did very badly in the subsequent General Election, but MacDonald continued as Prime Minister, overwhelmingly relying on Conservative / National support. The Labour Party expelled him. It was the King's personal

---

73   After taking soundings in the Party, but rejecting the most obvious candidate, R A Butler
74   Chamberlain continued as Party Leader

appointment; MacDonald was no longer Party Leader.

It was, therefore, a distinct possibility that Edward VIII could have chosen his own Prime Minister (ie Churchill), or at least made a very serious attempt to do so. But Baldwin was too clever for him.

Churchill did not succeed in becoming Leader of a King's Party, but Edward VIII might realistically have expected that he could appoint his own Prime Minister.

If Edward VIII had appointed Churchill as Prime Minister, Churchill would have found himself in a difficult position. Edward VIII could also have sacked him. Moreover, although Churchill readily abandoned 'principles' when it suited him, and changed sides, he was very much labelled as the man for rearmament (and probably war) against Germany. As the King wanted peace with Germany, it would have been an uneasy alliance. But it is interesting to speculate what might have happened if he had been appointed Prime Minister by Edward VIII. Churchill might well have been persuaded to go to war with Russia rather than Germany, as most of the Royal Family, business people, and the aristocracy would have preferred. The Americans would have been happy to manufacture armaments for any war. Britain and Germany might have become Allies, and might even have defeated communism[75].

Edward VIII would not easily be manipulated by the politicians. George VI was a very different character, but even he, at first, seemed to have an inflated idea of the king's power and position. On the very eve of war (on learning of the Nazi-Soviet Pact)

---

75   If Queen Elizabeth (King George VI's wife) was instrumental in deposing King Edward VIII, perhaps she really was 'the most dangerous woman in Europe'

The king's first thought was that he should appeal personally to Hitler, without delay, before the world was overtaken by calamity[76].

Chamberlain was able to prevail over George VI, but that did not stop the Duke of Windsor sending a personal telegram to Hitler, on 29 August 1939, urging him not to fight.

At the time, Churchill was writing *Marlborough: His Life and Times* – four large volumes published 1934-38. Marlborough (1659-1722) was an ancestor of Winston Churchill[77]. His full title was John Churchill, 1st Duke of Marlborough, Prince of Mindelheim, Prince of Mellenburg[78].

Marlborough served the Catholic Duke of York (King James II 1685-1688) in the 1670s and early 1680s. But he saw which way the wind was blowing, and switched sides to the Dutch Protestant William of Orange who became the monarch (jointly with his wife Mary) in February 1689[79]. Marlborough served them faithfully and with distinction for some years. But being someone who had changed sides, he was not fully trusted. (The same could be said of Winston Churchill two centuries later.) Marlborough was suspected of Jacobitism (favouring the old Catholic King across the water) and was temporarily imprisoned in the Tower. He reached his zenith in the reign of Queen Anne (1702-1714), particularly in the War of the Spanish Succession (1701-1714), at the battles of Blenheim (1704), Ramillies (1706), Oudenarde (1708) and Malplaquet (1709).

Blenheim Palace was built as a reward to Marlborough from a grateful nation in recognition of his military success. For many, his successes

---

76   Cadbury, p 88
77   Winston Churchill was a grandson of the 7th Duke of Marlborough
78   Diana, Princess of Wales (1961-1997), was also a descendant of his
79   William continued ruling alone until 1702; Mary died in 1694

established Britain[80] as a Great Power in Europe.

In the early eighteenth century, some Tories accused Marlborough of prolonging the War of the Spanish Succession for his own glory. The problem was keeping the Allies, who had different war aims, together. Eventually he was dismissed by the Tories, who concluded a Peace Treaty. Winston Churchill was determined that this should not happen to him. He was not a great military strategist, but he was a brilliant political operator. In the early years of the war Britain was short of resources, and had no allies in Europe. After that, he determinedly clung to his two very different allies: the USA and the Soviets. He also carefully protected his political position at home from those Tories and others who wanted to abandon him and conclude a separate peace.

Undoubtedly Winston Churchill was influenced by (his research on) his illustrious ancestor, who, in some ways, he sought to emulate. Marlborough was certainly highly ambitious for fame, wealth and glory, and was able to capitalise on his military and diplomatic skills to achieve all three. Churchill's skills were more with words – oratory and writing. He was aware that someone's reputation relies heavily on what is written about them, and was determined to redress the balance to restore the reputation of his famous ancestor. He did this by writing the biography of Marlborough, who had been criticised by Macaulay (a century earlier) and others. He was also determined to write his own history of himself and WW2, which he did effectively. For a whole generation, most people's assessments of Churchill relied heavily on what he had written about himself.

Both Marlborough and Churchill chose to change sides when they thought it was in their interest to do so. Marlborough strongly supported James II before he was King, but, when he saw that the Jacobite

---

80   Which included Scotland from 1706

ship was sinking, switched to supporting the Protestant William and Mary, who he helped to become King and Queen. Churchill was a Conservative supporter in the early years of the twentieth century, but when opinion moved against the Conservatives, he joined the Liberals in time to be a member of the 1906 Liberal Government. After WW1 he re-joined the Conservative Government, after briefly flirting with the label 'Constitutionalist'. As a result of changing sides, both men generated considerable mistrust.

Both the War of the Spanish Succession, and WW2 were extraordinarily expensive. Marlborough was fortunate: his war was financed by early National Debt arrangements – Government-backed securities that could be traded. Churchill's war had more serious financial difficulties that bankrupted the nation and left it in hock to the Americans.

But eventually each of them won the long-term gratitude of the British nation for success in war, whether real or apparent.

In his 1937 book *Great Contemporaries* Churchill said that he hoped that Hitler, despite his rise to power through dictatorial action, hatred and cruelty, might yet go down in history as the man who restored honour and peace of mind to the great Germanic nation, and brought it back serene, helpful and strong to the forefront of the European family circle. The restoring of honour to Germany implied the reversal of much of the Treaty of Versailles which was soon to cause so much trouble (See Chapter 2, part 3). But in the late 1930s Churchill was advocating rebuilding the British Air Force and strengthening the League of Nations, which could help prevent war. He was hardly consistent in his attitudes – however much he might subsequently claim otherwise.

Some explain that Churchill

Was a weathervane who said so many different things at different times that, in the words of Beaverbrook, he ended up holding all views on all questions. Or, as Asquith put it, 'Winston has no convictions'[81].

Chamberlain damned him with faint praise, when he said in the House of Commons:[82]

I have the greatest admiration for my right honourable friend's many brilliant qualities. He shines in every direction. I remember once asking a Dominion statesman... What in his opinion was the most valuable quality a statesman could possess. His answer was judgement. If I were asked whether judgement is the first of my Right Honourable friend's many admirable [83]qualities I would have to ask the House of Commons not to press me too hard

Baldwin[84] said of Churchill:

When Winston was born, lots of fairies swooped down on his cradle [with] gifts – imagination, eloquence, industry, ability, and then came a fairy who said 'No one person has a right to so many gifts', picked him up and gave him such a shake and a twist, that with all these gifts he was denied judgement and wisdom. That is why while we delight to listen to him... we do not take his advice[85].

According to Marr he was seen by most of the Establishment, and many Conservatives, as

---

81   Quoted by Johnson (who does not agree), p 157
82   Jenkins, p 536
83   Jenkins, p 511
84   Stanley Baldwin (1867-1947) Prime Minister 1923-24, 1924-29 and 1935-37
85   Jenkins, p 511

A rather ridiculous, drunken dodgy man with a penchant for wild speeches and silly hats. Behind their gloved hands they [called] him the 'rogue elephant' and even 'the gangster' ... in Labour circles, he was widely regarded as the enemy of the working class, the pink-faced toff who, years ago, had ordered the army in against the strikers[86].

Attlee agreed with Lloyd George's comment about Churchill:

... he's got ten ideas, and one of them is right, but he never knows which it is[87].

Churchill had a small group of supporters in the House of Commons, divorced from the Conservative Party leadership. He continued to campaign for re-armament, and opposed Chamberlain's appeasement policies. But his anti-Hitler pro-rearmament stance was not as consistent or long-term as many have since inferred. In May 1935 Churchill said of Hitler's latest peace offer:

...all must welcome the friendly tone on Herr Hitler, his friendly references to this country, and the several important points which he brought forward and which form a good basis on which conversations could perhaps be founded...We cannot tell whether Hitler would be the man who will once again let loose upon the world another war in which civilisation will inevitably succumb, or whether he will go down in history as the man who restored honour and peace of mind to the great German nation[88].

He was keeping his options open. In 1936 he had tried to make common cause with elements from the Labour and Liberal Parties who also dissented from the government's foreign policy. He was

---

86   Marr, p xv
87   Toye, p 380
88   Toye, p 316

....left politically isolated. Attlee kept his distance, as did Eden, and Churchill was left with the support of only a few maverick back-bench MPs such as Harold Macmillan and Bob Boothby, plus the Imperialist hardliners Leo Amery and Lord Lloyd, together with his old cronies such as Brendan Bracken[89].

After the Munich Agreement he said to Chamberlain, in the House of Commons:

You were given the choice between war and dishonour. You chose dishonour and you will have war.

That seems to be the settled view of history. When weighed against the terrible consequences of war (see Chapter 8), it is worth asking whether 'dishonour' might have been preferable. It is also worth asking what honour there was in giving a guarantee to Poland, and then dishonouring it. Britain gave no help to Poland at all; it was not very honourable to promise something which could not be delivered, and to have war as well. The idea that war was 'honourable' became a powerful myth. Churchill's original idea of 'war' may have been about chasing dark-skinned people on horseback in far-away countries, with no impact on people at home in Britain. Perhaps he did not foresee the terrible consequences of massive bombing of civilians and cities; still less did he foresee the horrors of the atomic bombs in Hiroshima and Nagasaki.

If he were applying for a job as Prime Minister and War Leader today, with his curriculum vitae he would probably not have been shortlisted. He did not do well at school in important subjects. He did not go to university. He struggled to gain admission to Sandhurst. He was an aristocrat, somewhat out of touch with ordinary people. Today he would be regarded as being mentally ill – he suffered

89   Ponting, *1940*, p 62

from depression (which he called 'black dog'), and if he was not an alcoholic, he was certainly dependent on alcohol. He was fat, not fit, and greedy. Within three months of the war beginning he would be an Old Age Pensioner. He was widely mistrusted, had changed his political party twice, and he had been in the political wilderness for 10 years. Many of his abilities were recognised: he was a master of the English language, and a brilliant orator. But his judgement, over a number of matters, was seriously in doubt. He had loved being a soldier, and had previously found that fighting in a war could help to restore his reputation.

He famously said 'History will be kind to me for I intend to write it', and it seems that his version of what happened in World War 2 has dominated (non-)thinking ever since. About his writing, Churchill also said:

This is not history. It is my case[90].

Churchill certainly wanted to make a name for himself, and he had some illustrious ancestors to live up to. The greatest was Marlborough, with whom Churchill was only too familiar. He also wanted to live up to his father's achievements: Lord Randolph Churchill (1849-95) had become Chancellor of the Exchequer at the age of 37; Churchill did not manage that until he was nearly 50.

Jenkins[91] relates a highly revelatory dream which Churchill had while he was painting. It was in 1947, after he had achieved most of his fame. In the dream, his father appeared. There was a long conversation between them in which Winston related all the changes that had taken place in the last half century. The father seemed to assume that Winston was a retired soldier, or a professional painter,

---

90   Jenkins, p 824
91   Jenkins, p 825

and was surprised by the signs of relative affluence. The father said

as I listened to you unfolding these fearful facts, you seemed to know a great deal about them ... when I hear you talk I wonder you didn't go into politics ... you might even have made a name for yourself.

It seems that the need to impress his father, and make a name for himself, still figured prominently in Churchill's subconscious mind, even when he was one of the most famous men in the world.

One might also wonder whether to Churchill it was more important to be a politician, and to make a name for himself, than to be a War Leader and to save Civilisation and Democracy from the Nazis – and whatever other 'principles' have since been attributed to him.

In 1939-40 Churchill was more prepared to become Prime Minister and War Leader than anyone else.

Of course Churchill did not cause WW2; nor was it started to further his political career. Neither was he a Marlborough, though both could be accused of prolonging a war for their own political reasons[92]. But the war did prove to be the saviour of his political career and the basis for his subsequent reputation – which rests on pro-war attitudes and on myths rather than reality. People seem to rally to the cries of patriotism, duty, jingoism and nationalism – in spite of associated deaths and destruction – rather than peace, friendship, compromise and co-operation. One of Churchill's achievements was to make 'appeasement' a term of abuse, and to discredit the search for peace rather than the pyrrhic victory of war. We are all losers in, and diminished by, War.

---

92   In late May 1940

Graham Sutherland's portrait of Churchill was presented to him by the House of Commons for his 80th birthday. He called it 'a remarkable example of modern art'. His wife, Clementine, always keen to protect his legacy, destroyed it because it did not portray the heroic, warrior statesman image that she wanted to protect.

Chapter 5
Alternatives

Hitler invaded Poland on September 1, 1939. Chamberlain reluctantly declared war on Germany on September 3, 1939, egged on by MPs and the press. His declaration was ostensibly in accordance with the ill-conceived and ill-fated Polish guarantee, outlined in Chapter 3. But to suggest that Britain went to war to help Poland is A BIG LIE: Britain did nothing to help Poland.

Britain was unable and/or unwilling to do anything to help Poland: it was too far away, Britain had not made the preparations that would have been necessary, and Hitler was too quick for Britain to respond effectively.

Actions (or inactions) speak louder than words. Britain and France (although they probably thought otherwise) were simply not strong enough to stand up to Germany in Poland.

Besides, Britain and France were to the west of Germany, and Poland was to the east. It was impractical to send any help, even if they had wanted to.

The only ways to have prevented a German invasion of Poland would have been either:

- Negotiation – but Poland was intransigent, they would yield nothing; or
- In alliance with Russia – but the Poles had put the kibosh on that. They wanted neither German nor Russian troops on their territory. But without a triple alliance (Britain, France and Russia) to help them, they ended up invaded by both Germany and Russia.

In any case, before invading, Hitler had been astute enough to line up an alliance with Russia for himself, whereby they divided Poland between the two of them; that virtually guaranteed that Russia and Germany would defeat Poland.

It is unlikely that French troops would have been any more successful (in 1939) at defending Poland than they were the following year at defending France, and no-one wanted to 'Die for Danzig'. Moreover, it would have been difficult to motivate British troops to fight (apparently hopelessly) when Britain (though not Poland) was willing to concede most of what Hitler wanted.

Chamberlain had already conceded that the Czechoslovakian crisis was: *A quarrel in a far away country between people of whom we know nothing*[93].

Perhaps he though the same about Poland, or even that Poland was somewhere handy, like Belgium! That was where he sent British troops (as if in preparation for the subsequent Dunkirk evacuation).

British troop movement was designed more to hem Germany in than it was to help Poland.

Churchill sent troops to Norway and subsequently to North Africa and Sicily – almost anywhere except Poland. That reveals more about British intentions (and relative weakness), than it does about their knowledge of Geography.

We should stop pretending that WW2 was to save Poland from Hitler: it was the pretext and the spark that started the war, just as the Assassination of Archduke Ferdinand was the pretext and the spark that ignited WW1.

---

93   27 September 1938

The story of WW2 is often told as if Britain's declaring war on Germany inevitably followed Hitler's invasion of Poland as surely as night follows day. But that did not have to be the case.

There are always alternatives to fighting a war, and war should be a last resort after all options have been explored. It may be difficult to evaluate the costs and benefits of any particular alternative, and predictions about future results are likely to be inaccurate. However, one can predict with reasonable certainty that a war will result in casualties, injuries, deaths, destruction and substantial other costs. There is no way of knowing whether or not these costs will be outweighed by any benefits that it is hoped will accrue from fighting a war.

Similarly, the outcome of alternatives other than war are uncertain. But, in war, as well as casualties, other unpredicted, unexpected or accidental outcomes may well occur. For example, few in the West joined WW2 with the intention of enabling Stalin to conquer most of Eastern Europe, but that was the result. In Britain, few favoured the war because it would bankrupt the country, and lead to the loss of Empire, but that was the result. Those who favoured the war did not expect that the results of the war would be so different from their intentions.

We cannot be certain what the outcomes of the suggestions in this chapter might have been, but they could hardly have been worse than the results of the actual war.

Doing nothing was an option that would have been less costly, less deadly[94] and less damaging than going to war. But there were other options which more serious effort could have made effective –

---

94   It might be objected that 'doing nothing' would have been deadly and costly to the Jews. But war did not save them, nor was it intended to

depending on what objectives were being pursued.

There were two principal occasions in 1939-40 when careful, rational consideration could have led to war being avoided:

A. The decision (by Chamberlain) to issue the Polish Guarantee (March 1939).
B. The decision (by Churchill), when he was first appointed as Prime Minister (in May 1940), to continue with war, when the British position seemed hopeless.

The world is full of relatively small nations that have had to learn to live in the shadow of more powerful, potentially threatening, larger nations. This is usually achieved by co-operation rather than confrontation, and avoiding being provocative.

When the decision was made to give the Polish Guarantee (or when the consequent decision to declare war, six months later, was made), no-one could really be sure what the consequences would be. History is sometimes written as if there were no alternative. Below, thirteen possibilities are examined that would have been better than all-out war. Perhaps no single one would have been totally effective[95], and there are always arguments against each. But no-one could be sure, any more than Chamberlain could know, what the results of his actions would be.

Although each 'Alternative' has been listed as if they were separate and different possibilities, some of them could be combined. For

---

95   Effective in achieving what? It is difficult to define what the objectives were of those pursuing the war. Defeating Hitler? Defeating the Nazis? Saving Poland? Saving the Jews? Stopping Germany from being top dog in Europe? Saving Civilisation, Democracy and Freedom? Saving, protecting or creating personal political positions and reputations?

example it would have been possible to negotiate without meeting Hitler (eg by telephone, or through diplomats or third parties), or to meet Hitler without negotiating. But it would have made more sense to do both at the same time.

1. Do Nothing

The main alternative to declaring war was, of course, not to declare war, or to do nothing. That would have been seen as betraying Poland and reneging on the Polish Guarantee. The British Press and MPs would have opposed that, and Chamberlain would not have survived as Prime Minister. And so he declared war, and then did nothing, or very little, and certainly nothing to help Poland. The 'phoney war' followed. The declaration of war seemed to be more about political necessity for Chamberlain's survival than it was about Poland's survival. The position was rather similar in May 1940, when Churchill first became Prime Minister – although Britain's position was hopeless (militarily and financially)[96], and a peace settlement was on offer, Churchill had to continue the war in order to survive politically: he had been appointed in order to fight the war, and that was his way of seeking fame, glory and honour.

The war was apparently the result of the Polish Guarantee and Hitler's invasion of Poland. But there were other factors at work. Clearly, Russia and Germany wanted to, and did, conquer Poland. But Britain and France had another agenda: they wanted to clip Germany's wings. Germany was becoming too big and too powerful, and was upsetting the balance of power in Europe.

The result of the Polish Guarantee was a disastrous war. The result

---

96   Britain could not continue the war without substantial financial and military assistance from America; in order to win, Russia's help was needed too

of not declaring war might have been that Hitler would have invaded the rest of Europe, Britain, the British Empire, the rest of the world, and have destroyed Freedom, Democracy and Civilisation. Much of the warmongers' propaganda suggested this, and it is still widely believed.

The world has plenty of unacceptable regimes that deny civil and human rights, carry out public executions, keep prisoners on death row for years, have detention without trial, persecute particular groups of citizens, dispute with their neighbours over borders, invade each other's territory, confiscate land and other property from their citizens, and persecute or enforce particular religions. But Britain does not go around declaring war on, and bombing, everyone with whom it disagrees, or offering guarantees to their neighbours. Most such wars would be unwinnable, and such guarantees would be unenforceable. So, mostly, and rightly, Britain does no more than protest.

But it is worth trying to assess what would have been most likely to have happened if Britain had done nothing. There would have been no Polish guarantee, and Hitler would have conquered Poland anyway. If Britain had respected Norway's neutrality, Hitler would have had no need to invade Denmark and Norway. He would have felt no need to defend his western front if Britain and France had not declared war on Germany – France, Belgium, the Netherlands, and Luxembourg would probably not have been invaded. Six million Jews might have been murdered anyway (but without war it would have been possible for more to emigrate). Germany and Russia would have fought each other, and exhausted each other. We do not know who would have won, but Eastern Europe would have been conquered by one or the other brutal dictator (Stalin or Hitler). Britain would not have been made bankrupt and become subservient to America. Eventually the Nazi regime would have collapsed anyway. The British Expeditionary Force would not have been left stranded in Dunkirk, losing most of its equipment, and the Dunkirk evacuation would not have been necessary.

Hitler had no intention of invading Britain until after Britain had declared war on Germany. Suggestions that he wanted to conquer the whole world and destroy civilisation are wholly misleading.

Another consequence of 'doing nothing' is that Churchill would not have achieved fame and glory. He would have been just another failed Tory MP, who no-one trusted: an effective writer, an eccentric who was incorrigible, shameless, and perhaps a genius. But he would have disappeared from History, and few would have heard of him today.

Of course most of the people of Eastern Europe did not want to submit to Germany (any more than they wanted to submit to the Soviet Union – although they had to as a result of war). Hitler may have thought of most of them as being of inferior races (eg Slavs and Jews), and assumed the right of the 'superior' Germans to rule over them.

The idea of a 'superior' race ruling over 'inferior 'races may well have been borrowed from Britain. Indeed, it was the basis of the British Empire. In Africa, India, and other parts of Asia, the British regarded it as proper for whites to rule over 'inferior' black- and brown-skinned people – at least Churchill did. He said:

I do not admit that a great wrong has been done to the Red Indians of America or the black people of Australia....by the fact that a stronger race, a higher grade race, a more worldly-wise race ... has come in and taken their place[97].

---

97 Speaking to the Peel Commission in 1937 justifying Britain deciding the fate of Palestine

Presiding over the near elimination of such races has comparisons with Hitler's racist activities – a comparison that would not have been lost on Hitler himself, who wanted his own European Empire, based on the supposed superiority of the Aryan race.

Churchill also said *I am strongly in favour of using poisonous gas against* **uncivilised tribes**[98].

He was also, for too long, in favour of retaining British rule in India:

I hate Indians. They are a beastly people with a beastly religion[99]

Perhaps Hitler's and Churchill's opinions on racial superiority were not unusual in that period. But Churchill cannot claim the high moral ground in this respect.

In sum the fascist attitude to socialists and Jews was not utterly different from the Imperialist attitude to Blacks... Hitler was the supremely disgusting example of something that was not so alien to the European mentality: the tendency to put different kinds of people into different sealed categories and then to treat them differently[100].

Both Hitler and Churchill were men of the nineteenth century who thought it was right that 'superior' races should rule over 'inferior' races. Churchill was as reluctant for the British to leave India as Hitler was determined not to leave Poland.

Hitler was not particularly keen on having a German Empire in Africa and other parts of the world. He wanted supremacy in Eastern Europe.

---

98   1920, regarding Iraqi revolutionaries, emphasis added
99   Quoted in Leo Amery's diaries, 1942
100 Calvocoressi, p 26-7

Of course the Jews could have been 'disposed of' more humanely, by facilitating, instead of blocking, their emigration to Britain, Palestine, the USA, the British Empire and the rest of the world. Clearly the Germans were keen to get rid of the Jews. But most nations were reluctant to take more than a few, and numbers were severely limited. If Britain had not declared war on Germany, Jews would have been freer to escape from dreadful conditions and to emigrate. But their routes were blocked by wartime restrictions.

'Doing Nothing' may sound complacent. But doing nothing is better than doing the wrong thing, or doing more harm than good.

2. Negotiation

If 'doing nothing' was unacceptable, a second possibility was negotiation. Churchill is often quoted as saying that 'jaw jaw is better than war war'[101]. But he would not negotiate with 'that man' (Hitler). The reason given for this is usually that Hitler could not be trusted. He had broken his word over Czechoslovakia, and there was no point in negotiating with him about anything else because he would break his word again. Other countries did not keep their word either[102].

He might promise anything, but cede nothing. Churchill also talked as if 'negotiation' meant surrender. Of course, as a master of the English language, Churchill knew exactly what he was doing in conflating the two ideas. He wanted to continue with the war, for whatever reasons, and wanted 'negotiation' to sound like surrender. Another reason for not negotiating was that it was not clear what the Allies (mainly Britain and France) wanted, and so negotiation would

---

101 A sentiment to which most would agree, but Churchill's actions suggest he thought otherwise
102 Britain did not keep its word over helping Poland, or proceeding with general disarmament

have been difficult; and whatever the Allies wanted[103] was most likely unobtainable.

Hitler was adamant over Eastern Europe, and would give up nothing. He was, however, more flexible over Western Europe. Negotiations might have led to his withdrawal from Norway, Denmark, Belgium, the Netherlands and France. Moreover, he might well have been willing to negotiate for the deportation of Jews, rather than their extermination. But Churchill would not even try. His political career and the glory of war were more important to him than the Jews.

Hitler was willing to allow continued independence, and the continuation of the British Empire – in return for either an alliance with Britain, or at least Britain's benevolent neutrality, to allow him a free hand in Eastern Europe. But Churchill wanted nothing less than total victory over Germany.

Churchill wanted and needed substantial assistance from America if Britain were to continue with the war. He could not let America see that negotiations and a respectable peace were possibilities. The evil of the Nazis had to be talked up as if they might even invade America. Any talk of negotiations might have led the Americans to believe that Britain would not continue with the war, and so there was no need to help. Saving France (and Belgium, the Netherlands, Denmark and Norway) from the Nazis, or saving a few (or a few million) Jews, were less important than getting American aid to continue with the war.

Most wars end with some negotiation (unless the aim is total defeat and humiliation), and it would be better if the negotiations could take place before the disasters of war rather than afterwards.

But negotiation had come to sound like appeasement, which soon

---

103 Probably to curtail Germany

had a nasty smell about it. Total victory over Germany was preferred, as in WW1, when the victors could rub the Germans' noses in the dirt, humiliate them and demand reparations. As we have seen, that approach led to a Second World War.

However, experience had also shown that negotiating with Hitler could delay his activities. For example, the German invasion of Poland was scheduled to begin at 4 am on Aug 26, 1939; but the British and the Poles were hinting to Berlin that they were willing to resume discussions. Hitler thought he may have been able to regain former German territory without the need for invasion; he therefore delayed the invasion for a few days. He even agreed that, in the future, Germany would help to defend the British Empire. Negotiation might have returned Danzig and the Polish Corridor to Germany, without fighting. Hitler could be delayed from going to war by the promise of negotiation.

The British Ambassador

Continued to believe that British pressure on Poland could avoid war... On August 31 he telegraphed to Lord Halifax (from Berlin) commenting that 'the German terms sound moderate to me... Poland... will never get such good terms again, guaranteed as they will be internationally'.[104]

Britain wanted to force Poland to open negotiations with Germany, but Poland would not.

Germany issued an ultimatum. The Polish ambassador did not have full signing powers, and so the Germans would not negotiate with him. Germany then invaded Poland.

Poland had refused to negotiate. British policy was to try to force

---

104 Gilbert, p 256

negotiations.

If France and Britain had been serious about defending Poland, protracted negotiations could have enabled them to put themselves in a better position to do so.

Of course, Poland did not want to submit to German demands. But, by negotiation, they could have secured a better position than they actually did. War, and the British guarantee, did the Poles more harm than good.

Negotiations with Hitler may not have been very hopeful, but negotiations might have been effective with other countries in producing alliances that had a more realistic prospect of deterring Hitler.

It seems strange that Churchill was unable to find European allies in the early years of the war (after the fall of France), if the Nazis were really the aggressors that he portrayed, threatening to invade everyone. If Eastern European countries along with Scandinavia and the Low Countries had stood together with Britain and France, that might have been enough to deter Hitler from invading Poland. Perhaps they thought Britain was an unsuitable ally, or did not trust Churchill, or did not believe his propaganda. Or perhaps they simply did not want another war.

In a radio broadcast in January 1940 Churchill urged the Dutch, Belgians and Scandinavians to

stand together with the British and French Empires against aggression and wrong.[105]

---

105   Roberts, p 84

But they did not. Perhaps quiet diplomacy could have achieved more than Churchill's grandstanding. It is not clear why Britain was unable to find allies in Europe. Perhaps they did not believe all the anti-German propaganda. Perhaps they did not want to volunteer to be attacked by Germany. Churchill's appeal to those countries may have served only to provoke Hitler. Until early 1940 Hitler still considered Norway's neutrality to be the best course for Germany. He was dependent on iron ore from neutral Sweden; for much of the year it could be shipped via the Baltic. But in winter, the Baltic Sea was frozen, and it had to travel via Norway. And when Hitler heard that Britain intended to violate Norway's neutrality, to block the iron ore shipments, he resolved to get there before the British[106]. Churchill himself had leaked the gist of British intentions in Scandinavia[107] whereas Hitler's daring and effective plans were kept secret before being successfully implemented[108].

Negotiation, rather than declaring war, could have delayed the war, enabled more effective alliances to be built, and produced a better outcome for Poland.

3. Meeting with the Enemy

Although Churchill never met Hitler, he recognised that

Those who have met Herr Hitler face-to-face in public business or on social terms have found a highly competent, cool, well-informed functionary with an agreeable manner, and a disarming smile, and few have been

---

106 Roberts, p 84
107 The result was that the British were humiliated in Norway, leading to the resignation of Chamberlain as Prime Minister. This led to Churchill becoming Prime Minister, but there is no evidence that he deliberately manipulated the Norway disaster with this objective in mind.
108 Roberts, p 84

unaffected by a subtle personal magnetism[109].

It seems strange that Churchill, who would willingly, at the drop of a hat, cross the Channel, or Europe, or the Atlantic for meetings with the French, Russian or American leaders in pursuit of peace, did not meet Hitler. In response to one of Hitler's peace offers, Churchill said:

I do not propose to say anything in response to Herr Hitler's speech, not being on speaking terms with him [110].

A meeting might have facilitated a negotiated peace, but Churchill did not want that. A chat over a cup of tea or coffee[111], with some human warmth, and recognition of each other's interests and needs, might have done more good than fighting, killing and bombing.

We can only speculate why they did not meet. Churchill would have been unwilling to defer to Hitler, as he did to Stalin and Roosevelt. He was also very susceptible to flattery and amiability, which may have been forthcoming from Hitler. At the end of the war, he was, according to Colville[112]

overjoyed by 'a nice telegram from Stalin, indeed the most friendly [he]has ever sent'. His [Churchill's] vanity was astonishing ... and I am glad that [Stalin] does not know what effect a few kind words... might well have upon our policy towards Russia.

Churchill may have feared that he would be charmed by Hitler. At the end of his premiership Colville advised Eden:

---

109 Churchill, W S, *Great Contemporaries* 1935 and later editions
110 Roberts, p 143
111 Although such beverages would not have been strong enough for Churchill
112 Jenkins, p 787-8

Amiability must be the watchword: the Prime Minister thrived on opposition and show-downs, but amiability he could never resist[113].

International meetings and diplomacy are intended to increase international understanding and reduce suspicion. According to Lloyd George

International suspicion is at the root of... some of the worst evils. Nations, like dogs, are always convinced that the other dog is out to steal their bone... Much of our world trouble has arisen from national misunderstanding and suspicion ...However much man has progressed individually ...internationally he is still in the canine stage[114].

Britain thought it was 'top dog' and would not lower itself to speaking to a parvenu like Hitler from a new and newly over-aggrandised nation.

Amiability in international relations is better than war. But Churchill was determined to continue with the war, to the end, in the hope of total victory, and to secure his place in history.

4. Issuing no Guarantees

Churchill's decision to continue with the War in May 1940 was a key decision point. Another was in March 1939 when Chamberlain's government issued the ill-fated and foolish (See Chapter 3) Polish Guarantee. It was that Polish Guarantee (March 31, 1939), and Hitler's invasion of Poland, which led Britain to declare war on Germany (Sept 3, 1939), but Britain did little or nothing to honour that guarantee.

As it meant so little in practice, it would have been more honest to give

---

113 Jenkins, p 895
114 Gilbert, p 76

no guarantee. Britain declared war on Germany because of the Polish Guarantee; eventually Poland was saved from that wicked dictator Hitler, only to be given to that wicked dictator Stalin. That was hardly success, and it became possible to defeat Hitler only because of two strokes of luck: (i) the Japanese bombed Pearl Harbor, which brought America into the war. Britain alone could not have defeated Germany. (ii) Hitler over-extended his troops by invading Russia; the Russians, in turn, invaded Poland and Germany. At first WW2 was an enormous gamble for Britain, which had little chance of winning. But once America and Russia joined in against Germany, the balance of power changed completely.

The Polish Guarantee had been intended to deter a German invasion. It did not. It served only to raise expectations in Poland – which were soon shattered. It has also been much misunderstood: it did not guarantee Poland's borders; nor did it promise protection for every part of the country that was invaded. But Britain chose to respond by declaring war on Germany – supposedly to deter Germany from further conquests. But it gave those who were keen on war a justification for declaring war.

The phrase 'the guilty men' has often been applied to the 'Appeasers', Chamberlain and others. It might more realistically be applied in respect of those same men who issued the worthless guarantee to Poland. [In relation to the Munich Agreement] Churchill said, 'England has been offered a choice between war and shame. She has chosen shame and will get war'. Chamberlain and Churchill preferred the shame of betraying Poland, and being responsible for the killing of hundreds of thousands, rather than have 'England's' pride, honour and glory tarnished.

It may even be that it was the issue of the Polish guarantee that provoked Hitler to invade Poland. It may have seemed that his neighbours, both to the east and to his west, were conspiring against Germany.

It was a mistake to issue the Polish guarantee, and similar guarantees to Greece and Romania. It seems unlikely that many people seriously thought that Britain would somehow transport troops to Poland and Eastern Europe and provide fighting support. It would have been very difficult without going via German land, or German controlled sea; flying would be impracticable; going via the Mediterranean would be too time-consuming; and, indeed, Britain did not.

The French and British provided a little help, briefly, by creating a western front, so that Germany had to fight on two fronts, and Britain sent its Expeditionary Force to help with that. But they lost, hopelessly, and soon had to withdraw, without Germany having to withdraw troops from the east. This demonstrated that it was impractical and unrealistic to 'guarantee' Poland, once Germany invaded (especially as Germany collaborated with Russia in this).

5. Rescuing Jews

If it was unacceptable to do nothing, and there was no effective way of negotiating or creating alliances, and the enemy regime was so awful that 'something had to be done', it would be necessary to examine other options. In the years after WW2 it was generally accepted that the Nazis, responsible for the Holocaust, had to be eliminated, whatever the cost. But that was not an argument for starting the war in 1939, when the Holocaust[115] had not even begun. It was well known that the Germans treated the Jews badly, but the horrors of the Holocaust were not widely known about until some years later. It was clear that, in the 1930s, Germany treated its Jews badly with persecution and worse; but there was anti-Semitism in many countries, including Britain; and countries like Poland and Russia were hardly better than Germany. If there was a case for war

---

115 The Holocaust and the intention to kill all Jews on an industrial scale in death camps

against Germany for their treatment of the Jews in the 1930s, there was perhaps also a case for war against other countries too. Declaring war on Germany helped neither the Poles nor the Jews[116].

Many Jews escaped from Germany and Eastern Europe before the war, for example to Britain, America and Palestine. Nearly ten thousand children escaped to Britain from the Nazis through 'kindertransport' with the help of the British Government and various remarkable volunteers. One of those, who eventually became well-known, was Nicholas Winterton. He found homes in Britain for over 600 children and arranged trains via the Netherlands to take them there. The last train left Prague on 3 September 1939, but was sent back because the war had started. Britain declared war on Germany on 3 September 1939. Nearly all of the children on that train were subsequently killed. Declaring war certainly did not help those particular children, and there is no knowing how many other Jews would have been able to emigrate, but for the war.

The war itself obviously made things more difficult. But large numbers of Jews did not seem to be welcome anywhere. Numbers were restricted in America. In Palestine there were objections from Arabs, many of whom rioted and resorted to violence.

Finally in May 1939 there came a White Paper promising the end of Jewish immigration after a further 75,000 Jews had been admitted ... the British Government had made repeated promises to the Jews. Now the promises were broken – too difficult to carry out, too expensive and worrying[117].

Most other countries seemed reluctant to take in Jews who were

---

116   The American invasion of Germany in 1945 saved about 100,000 Jews who remained in the concentration / death camps. It was no help to the 6,000,000 who had already been killed
117   A J P Taylor, *Oxford*, p 407

escaping from the Nazis before the war.

The uncertainties facing those in search of an escape from German racial policy was highlighted in June [1939] when 927 German-Jewish refugees sailed from Hamburg on board the ocean liner St Louis, *bound for the New World. The United States immigration quota numbers, which 734 of the refugees possessed, were not valid for another three years. Despite steaming within sight of the Florida coast, the refugees failed to persuade the United States Government to let them in. Twenty two were allowed to land in Cuba... [then] the Cuban Government ordered the ship to leave ... The Columbian, Paraguayan, Argentinian and Chilean Governments declined to open their doors to the refugees.*

The ship returned to Antwerp where more than 600 disembarked, going to areas that came to be ruled by Germany. Only 240 of them survived the war.[118]

The Jews had more than enough to cope with without obstacles being put in the way of emigration. There were many other parts of the world to which their emigration could have been facilitated.

But helping such Jews seemed to have an even lower priority once the war had begun, and obstacles were often put in the way of fleeing Jews (America severely restricted numbers, as did the British in Palestine – which they controlled).

The number of prisoners, especially Jews[119], steadily increased. But having a large number of prisoners (of a particular racial group) does not constitute a case for war and bombing. In recent years the country with by far the highest proportion of the population in prison, with a

---

118 Gilbert, p 248-9
119 Communists, homosexuals, opponents of the Nazis and others

particularly high number of a particular race[120], is the USA. But very few regard the USA as a particularly cruel regime, or declare war on them.

Unfortunately, rescuing the Jews was never a high priority for Britain and her allies. Even before the war started, *Kristallnacht* (9-10 Nov 1938) and the anti-Semitic terror were alerting British opinion. But Chamberlain was more concerned about British opinion than he was about the Jews. His unemotional pragmatism led him to propose to confine action to the relief of Jewish suffering in order to 'ease the public conscience'[121].

Churchill (and Britain)'s priority was to win the war 'at all costs' – even if the cost meant the murder of millions of Jews – which could have been prevented. Most people knew nothing of the Holocaust – the industrial scale murder of the Jews – until the end of the war, when the death camps were liberated and the Nuremberg Trials brought the horrors to everyone's attention. The British people could then bask in a glow of self-righteousness: Hitler had been so evil that it had been right to fight him, and all the sacrifice had been worthwhile. And as most British people did not know about the Holocaust, there was nothing they could have done. But getting rid of Hitler was a good thing, and the British could not be accused of standing idly by and watching millions being killed. They simply did not know.

But there was no excuse for Churchill and other political leaders: they did know.

If the Allies had any intention of taking significant action to save the Jews, it should have been done in the early years of the war, before six million were killed. They definitely knew.

---

120 Blacks
121 Self, p 345

On December 12 [1941]... the Allies issued a solemn declaration in London, Washington and Moscow, denouncing the mass murder of the Jews... [And] in condemnation in the strongest possible terms of what it called this bestial policy of **cold-blooded extermination**[122].

News of the Holocaust, the industrial scale killing of Jews (mainly in German controlled Poland) had come out in dribs and drabs and was not always believed (indeed, it was incredible that such things could happen), and it did not suit Britain to prioritise help to millions of Jews, and some of the news that came to Britain could be dismissed as Polish propaganda.

But the British Government could not plead total ignorance before 1944-45.

On 24 August 1941, in a radio broadcast, Churchill said:

whole districts are being exterminated. Scores of thousands – literally scores of thousands of executions in cold blood – are being perpetrated by German police troops ... Since the Mongol invasions in the sixteenth century, there has never been methodical, merciless butchery on such a scale, or approaching such a scale.

Churchill was reluctant to disclose all he knew about the killings because he did not want to alert the Germans to the fact that he was intercepting their secret messages. But in November 1941, Churchill wrote in the Jewish Chronicle: 'None has suffered more cruelly than the Jew'.

On 25 June 1942 *The Daily Telegraph* reported 50,000 Jews being slaughtered in Vilnius (in German occupied Lithuania), that the Germans were planning to murder all Jews, and that mobile gas

---

122 Gilbert, p 477, emphasis added

chambers were in use.

On 10 July 1942 *The Times* (London) reported on the liquidation of Poles and 'the most terrible situation of the Jews'.

In the summer of 1942 Ernst Lemmer reported on mobile and stationary gas chambers.

On 30 July 1942 Sydney Silverman (Labour MP) received a report on the proposed extermination of the Jews by prussic acid. There were also reports that they were to be electrocuted. Such reports were easily dismissed as being unreliable or from biased sources.

On 7 December 1942, *The Times* (London) reported that E Racsynski (Polish Foreign Minister) had passed proof of mass murder to Anthony Eden. Eden said that he had little doubt that a policy of gradual extermination of all Jews was being carried out by the Germans, and in the House of Commons on 17 December he referred to 'this bestial policy of cold-blooded extermination'.

Helping the Jews, as a main objective, would certainly have been worthwhile, and it would have been easier, cheaper, and quicker to make it effective than it was to fight an all-out war to the end. Churchill was a master with words; but actions (or inaction) should speak louder than words.

The possibility that Hess's mission to Britain brought proposals to save the Jews, which Churchill hushed up, is explored in Chapter 7.

In some countries, many brave individuals saved dozens or scores of Jews; some voluntary organisations saved hundreds; some Governments saved thousands. But nothing was done for the millions who perished. The usual argument is that it was better to achieve total victory, then the Nazi atrocities would be stopped. But total victory took a very long time, and millions perished waiting for a rescue that came too late.

Britain could and should have made a priority of rescuing Jews; perhaps offering to resettle all those who wanted, in the Dominions, or Africa, or other colonial territories, or even Palestine. Many had managed to escape from the Nazis before the war. But the fact is that Britain did not enter the war to rescue (many) Jews. The death camps did not even exist in 1939; the suggestion that Britain was conducting the war to save the Jews did not arise until the end of the war.

Very few trusted Hitler, and that was sometimes used as an excuse for not negotiating with him. If he had 'promised' to be kind to the Jews, no-one would have believed him. He might have agreed to allow free passage of Jews, especially if offered some inducements[123]. If he then did not deliver on his promises, the inducements would not have been delivered. In other words, negotiations could have been made effective, and there was nothing to be lost by trying.

It is even possible that, as Germany and Hitler's position became steadily weaker, and as any moderating influence from Hess had been eliminated, Hitler took it out on the Jews even more. Certainly deportation became more difficult with the war, and without co-operation from Britain. Churchill's rhetoric may have increasingly backed Hitler into a corner, and made the treatment of the Jews worse. We cannot know.

Serious consideration was given to bombing Auschwitz, or at least the railway lines running to it. But bombing was not particularly accurate. It might have been possible to save those who had not yet arrived

---

123 Perhaps the return of some former German colonies. Some other territories, in the Mediterranean or North Africa, were also sometimes regarded as negotiable

there, by killing a few hundred or thousand who were already there (and about to die anyway). But Churchill wanted to win the land war.

If the Allies had published what they knew about the killing of Jews, international pressure and rescue attempts could have saved many Jews. It could even have changed opinions amongst Germans, most of whom probably knew nothing of the Holocaust.

But, for Churchill, secrecy, and winning at all costs, were paramount.

It was as if British policy was to say to the Jews: 'Don't worry. We know these Nazis are a nasty lot and are persecuting and killing you. But we'll stop all that when we win the war. Just hang on for another five years. Unfortunately millions of you will be killed whilst waiting for some action to save you.'

6. Assassinate the Enemy

In a war situation, the propaganda is often highly personalised. Sometimes it seemed that WW2 was fought more against Hitler than it was against Germany or the Nazis. If Hitler, personally, was the real enemy, it should have been easier to kill one man than to defeat a whole nation.

At first Hitler gained some nationalist popularity by regaining some of what was lost at the Treaty of Versailles; he had helped to restore German pride after humiliation; and he tackled the economic problems that arose from the Depression, unemployment and hyperinflation. There was no overwhelming desire in Germany to get rid of him, and he was welcomed in Austria and elsewhere. But gradually the horrors of war started to catch up with him and he became increasingly dependent on a police state, the Gestapo, spies, informers and the apparatus of a dictatorship, with enemies being thrown into concentration camps.

The number of assassination attempts on Hitler steadily increased, but he was always carefully protected by trusted guards, and made sure that most of his movements were unpredictable, so that it was difficult to plan and implement an assassination attempt. Nevertheless, there were many such attempts over the years.

Churchill was keen on portraying the war as being a very personal dispute with Hitler. In Britain the war was pursued with vigour, ingenuity and determination on some unlikely fronts with a huge variety of efforts, contributions (eg garden railings and housewives' pots) and inventions, but there is little evidence of any serious effort by the Allies to assassinate Hitler. There were dozens of attempts on Hitler's life by a variety of nutcases, senior military officers, social misfits and others within Germany. These attempts were, of course, all unsuccessful. Those who tried, and failed, were usually soon executed.

But assassinating Hitler was not impossible. The 20 July 1944 plot did succeed in setting off a bomb, and injuring Hitler (which may have had continuing adverse effects on him); it also resulted in many executions – and disclosed the fact that he wore long underpants!

But danger and difficulty did not normally deter Churchill from doing what he thought needed to be done. The Special Air Service (SAS) was available to undertake dangerous and difficult tasks. It was originally conceived as a commando force to operate behind enemy lines in North Africa. Their first mission had been a disaster: one third of the unit (22 men) were killed or captured. Their second mission was a success (destroying 60 aircraft in Libya without loss). It was reconstituted and fought in Sicily and Greece, and towards the end of the war, in Belgium, the Netherlands and eventually Germany. In these last missions, 34 and then 32 men were summarily executed. It is clear that Britain had the capacity to risk dangerous assassination attempts on Hitler, if they had the intention.

There were reasons why Britain made no serious attempt to assassinate Hitler:

i. There was a fear that if Hitler were assassinated he would have been replaced by someone similar, perhaps someone more effective.

ii. The war was more against Germany and the Nazis, rather than Hitler personally.

World War 2 is often portrayed as if the problem was one very wicked man. If that was the case, the solution to the problem was simple (if difficult): get rid of him.

7. Involve League of Nations

In the modern world it is not acceptable for Country A to condemn Country B's regime and then declare, or wage war on Country B. International approval, preferably through the United Nations, is needed to legitimise war.

In the 1930s, the League of Nations was the predecessor of the United Nations. It had been created after WW1 in a rash of idealism (for peace, to prevent war and to settle international disputes; the idealism of some even favoured the adoption of the international language Esperanto). Britain and Poland were both members and had agreed, in international affairs, to submit complaints to the League for arbitration or judicial enquiry before going to war. By side-stepping this, Britain had chosen the old way (of nationalist wars) rather than following new idealistic agreements intended to avoid war; they chose war rather than civilised[124] behaviour.

The League had three sanctions:

i.   They could call on the states in dispute to sit down and discuss the problem in an orderly and peaceful manner, and verbally warn the offending country. If this failed they could

ii. Apply economic sanctions to force the offender into economic difficulties. If these failed, they could

iii. Apply physical sanctions, using military force. But the League had no troops of its own and had to rely on major nations like Britain and France. (Russia and Germany had not been allowed to join the League initially, but each became members for a few years in the 1930s; America did not join.)

It could be argued that all this would have been time consuming and would not have worked, and that it was OK for Britain and France to declare war straight away. But Britain could not claim the high moral ground if it did not attempt to do things properly.

Economic sanctions were not given much chance, but clearly Germany's position would have been seriously weakened if their access to oil and iron ore had been restricted. Imports of Sweden's iron ore was so important to Germany that Churchill violated Norwegian neutrality in a botched attempt to stop them. Hitler would have preferred Norway to remain neutral, but he was provoked into invading. There was also the possibility of making oil sanctions

---

124 Churchill is sometimes credited with saving 'civilisation'. But he preferred old-fashioned wars to civilised behaviour through the United Nations. His version of 'civilisation' is very different from what we would expect today

effective; tanks and planes cannot run on fresh air.

The destruction of the evils of Nazism was one result of the war. Another result was reaffirmation and validation of the practice of settling disputes by nationalistic wars rather than by peaceful international diplomacy and agreement. Nationalistic wars have dogged the world ever since.

8. Accept Reality

The reality was that Germany had been the biggest and most powerful nation in Europe[125] probably since 1871, and wanted to be recognised as such. Britain and France (with the help of the USA) had tried to put her in her place at the end of WW1, but she had risen again, and was fighting against humiliation. If only the British, and Churchill in particular, had been able to accept Germany as a Great Nation, much of the rivalry and fighting could have been avoided.

In some ways it might have been better if Britain had lost the First World War: there would have been no Treaty of Versailles to humiliate Germany, no Hitler to try to redress the balance, and no WW2. In WW1 Britain wanted total humiliation of Germany; they learned nothing from the 'success' of this misguided policy.

9. Democratic Solution

Churchill claimed to be fighting for democracy, but that may have been more of a War Cry to encourage support than it was reality. His position as a democratically elected Prime Minister was dubious. He is well known for saying that Democracy is the worst form of government, except for all those other forms that have been tried

---

125 Or at least in Central and Western Europe. The Soviet Union was not really a Great Power until the end of WW2

from time to time[126]. He also said that the best argument against democracy is a five minute conversation with the average voter.

With regard to the 1935 General Election, Churchill is recorded as saying:[127]

It is a fearsome thing to cast the whole future of the Empire on the franchise of so many simple folk.

Churchill's background was as an aristocrat and not as a democrat; he was brought up before one person one vote was accepted. In the UK, universal suffrage for men, and for women over 30, did not exist until 44 years after he was born[128]. He did not have the respect for 'average voters' that politicians have to show today. He was almost contemptuous of them. If he thought War was necessary (whether for the country or Europe or the world; or for his political career), he would go ahead, whatever his constituents thought[129].

Churchill had not been elected as Prime Minister[130]. The last General Election before the war was in 1935; the next was in 1945. He was elected as a Conservative MP in 1935; and that General Election resulted in a Conservative Government. But Churchill was not elected as a member of that Government – indeed he had fallen out with it, and was 'in the wilderness'. When support for Chamberlain as Prime

---

126 Hansard, Nov 11, 1947
127 Charmley, p 296-7
128 Votes for all women began 54 years after he was born; the elimination of multiple voting was 74 years after he was born
129 Indeed, his constituents in Epping came close to deselecting him as a candidate for this reason, before war broke out
130 Churchill was not elected as Prime Minister until 1951; even then the Labour Party had more votes than the Conservatives, and it was the quirkiness of the British electoral system that gave the Conservatives more seats

Minister waned (in 1940), Churchill was appointed as Prime Minister, by the King, on Chamberlain's recommendation.

Before the outbreak of war, it was clear that most people preferred Peace. There were too many bitter memories of the slaughter of WW1. When Chamberlain returned from Munich (1938) with a promise of Peace, he was enthusiastically received by large crowds, and Press and Parliament were overwhelmingly favourable. After Hitler invaded Czechoslovakia and Poland, and war was declared, people rallied around the Government and supported the war. As more and more was sacrificed (including deaths, injuries, and homes and cities bombed), there was an increasing desire to see that it was not all in vain, and to 'win' at all costs.

Whether or not Churchill, and The War, could have won an election would have depended on the timing. There was certainly plenty of opposition to him. He had fallen out with most of the Conservative Establishment; Chamberlain would have preferred the Foreign Secretary, Halifax, to succeed him (but he did not want to); early public opinion polls showed Eden as the preferred candidate; and during the war Churchill's Government had difficulty winning any by-elections that arose.

It was ordinary people, not the aristocracy, who bore the brunt of the war: the bombing, the fighting, the killing and being killed, the shortages, the rationing, and the loss of their homes. It was the aristocracy who decided what was 'best' for them.

Although it is sometimes argued that WW2 was fought to save democracy, the argument is difficult to sustain. Churchill was a democrat in that he was accountable to Parliament, but his appointment as War Leader was no more democratic than Hitler's[131]. Most countries in central and eastern Europe were not democracies, yet some became allies of Britain, whilst Germany was the enemy. Britain's going to war with Germany was nothing to do with democracy. If Britain had wanted Germany to become a democratic country, bombing the hell out of them would not do much good.

10. Befriend the Enemy

It was Jesus Christ who said that you should love your enemies and bless them who curse you and do good to them that hate you (Matthew 5:44), although many Christians forget their principles when there is the prospect of a good war.

Churchill himself did not claim to be a Christian, although he sometimes claimed that he was fighting for Christian principles.

Religious principles are not just woolly idealism. Over the centuries they have been found to be sensible and practical. When two people argue with each other, they can easily become more extreme, both in what they say themselves, and in what they allege their opponent has said. But if they each try to understand the other, (rather than trying to score points off each other and increasing misunderstanding and enmity) their positions are likely to come closer together, and there is usually more chance of influencing the behaviour of a friend than there is of influencing an opponent.

Serious international discussions and disclosure, rather than secrecy, warmongering and pushing the opponent to extremes might have had some influence on the worst aspects of the Nazi regime. It might have saved some Jews. It might have been a small step towards making

---

131 Hitler was the leader of the largest party in recent elections; Churchill was not

the world a better place by prioritising discussion and understanding over warmongering.

But we live in a world where, too often, the major powers see the answer to violence as being more violence. But, as is popularly said, violence begets violence. If A is violent to B, then B is violent to A; each side becomes more extreme and blames the other side. Each side comes to hate the other more, and peaceful settlement becomes more difficult. One war seems only to lead to another war; it does not prevent more wars. As Jesus Christ said, 'Those who use the sword shall die by the sword' (Matthew 26, 52). The answer to violence is not more violence. Peace and Love seem to be out of fashion when they are most needed. Talk and propaganda from warmongers help to undermine more humane attitudes of peace, love, understanding, and co-operation.

11. Defined and Limited Objectives

A war with defined and limited objectives might have been better, and have involved less suffering, than fighting to the death. But it is difficult to say what the Objectives of WW2 were. Different countries and different people had different objectives.

Hitler offered peace when he had conquered Poland. This was rejected by Britain – which chose to carry on fighting. But why? Many wanted to settle on reasonable terms with Hitler, but they were pledged to the defence of Poland – which they could not fulfil. It was not clear what was the objective of the war.

Did the British Government seek to overthrow fascism throughout Europe?, to destroy Germany as a great power?, or merely to substitute Goering or some other Nazi for Hitler as dictator of Germany? They did not know, and the British people were more or less told that they should not ask such questions[132].

Some of the suggestions in this Chapter might not have been effective. But, to be effective, an action needs to achieve defined objectives. And nations cannot have objectives; only individuals and groups can have objectives. Similarly, a war cannot have objectives of its own, but its participants can. And different people have different objectives. Some people in Britain supported the Soviet Union; some supported Nazism. Perhaps most people opposed both. Presumably most wanted to survive, keep their homes, and maintain a reasonable standard of living.

The objectives and intentions of leading politicians are harder to define. No doubt there were some idealists who put principle before their personal interest. For others, their personal position, power base and reputation were more important. And history is littered with examples of politicians, in Europe and elsewhere, who enhanced their position through a successful war (often disregarding the cost).

A politician who wants to enhance his or her position through war is unlikely to argue that they think waging war is a good thing, or that they like killing people, or that a good war will enhance their position and reputation. They are likely to say that they are fighting a defensive war and/ or for some 'principle', such as freedom, democracy, national interest, Christianity or even 'civilisation' itself.

Churchill was in favour of total victory at all costs. He said

If this long island history of ours is to end, let it end only when each of us lies choking in his own blood upon the ground[133]. Some might have accepted this colourful, romantic view of the future of Britain. Others might

---

132 A J P Taylor, *Oxford History*, p 458
133 Roberts, p 120

have preferred to live (and even to allow Germans to live).

After the war, as if to justify having 'won' the war, the idea that the war was to save the Jews became popular. But it was not true:

i. It did not save the Jews, or not many of them.[134] If saving the Jews had been a significant objective in WW2, significant and effective attempts to achieve this objective would have been made.

ii. Very little priority was given by the Allies to saving the Jews during the war. Most countries retained strict immigration restrictions. And there was some anti-Semitism among the Allies.

iii. The Nazis did not begin killing Jews on an industrial scale until about 1941, and it was not widely known or believed until 1944-45. Saving them could not have been a war objective when Britain declared war in 1939.

In 1939 the justification for Britain (and others) declaring war was Hitler's invasion of Poland, and the British and French guarantee for Poland. But if saving Poland had been a primary objective of the war, a more serious attempt to achieve that objective would have been made. Some money may have been loaned to Poland; French and British forces created a Western Front so that Germany would have to fight on two fronts. But it failed hopelessly. They did not intervene directly in Poland; they did not save Polish independence; and in the end, Poland was handed to the Russians.

The British aim was to stop German expansionism (which had been mainly, but not entirely, to regain what they had lost twenty years

---

134 Liberation in 1945 saved thousands in concentration camps who were awaiting their fate. It did nothing for the millions who had already met theirs.

previously at the end of WW1). They (British foreign policy) wanted to preserve some sort of balance of power so that Europe was not dominated by a single country. The result of going to war was that Germany dominated Europe for a few years, then much of Europe was given to the Soviets for them to dominate.

It is difficult to see what limited and achievable objective Britain might have had in 1939.

12. Sanctions

In the post war world international sanctions have sometimes been used to achieve particular objectives, and to avoid the horrors of war. They have of course not always been effective, and some seem to prefer going to war. But they have also been effective, for example in helping to end minority white rule in South Africa and Southern Rhodesia (Zimbabwe). Sanctions need to be applied thoroughly, with international cooperation. A world where nations cooperate to achieve progress is more civilised than one where international wars are regarded as acceptable.

Blockades intended to starve a nation to death are hardly civilised, yet both sides attempted this in WW2. More effective sanctions would have been, for example, to stop iron ore supplies from Sweden, and to stop supplies of oil from Rumania. Churchill's Norway Campaign for the former was a muddle and a disaster[135]; bombing oil supply facilities from Rumania, though inaccurate, were partially successful towards the end of the war. But American (Standard Oil) supplies continued through Switzerland. To be effective, sanctions need to be carefully planned, and watertight. Half-hearted sanctions never work. And we should always be wary of those who say the right thing, but find ways of doing the wrong thing.

---

135   So bad that Churchill replaced Chamberlain because of it!

13. Hearts and Minds

Hitler's regime could not have survived for long without a good deal of support from the German people. If Britain had put more effort into winning the hearts and minds of the German people, they could have helped to undermine the regime. Some unsuccessful efforts were made at a 'confetti war' – dropping propaganda leaflets over Germany. But they were not well enough designed or effective, and may have done more harm than good. Lloyd George said that dropping imbecile tracts over Germany could only have increased the morale of the German people[136]. A more carefully planned and sustained campaign, with more appropriate leaflets that Germans could believe, rather than dismissing them as propaganda, might have been effective. Churchill was very effective in convincing the British people of the evils of Nazism. It is a pity he could not undermine the Nazi position by convincing the Germans. Most Germans knew nothing of the worst excesses of the Nazis: they were kept secret. Churchill knew and should have done more to expose them. It seems that winning the war at all costs was a greater priority than winning the hearts and minds of the German people.

14. Accept Defeat

Although Britain was not threatened with invasion until after declaring war on Germany, a number of other nations were invaded and defeated. Churchill liked to portray invasion as being The End, saying that without victory there is no survival, and advocating fighting to the death. Some countries fought and lost and suffered badly with much bombing, deaths and destruction. Others reluctantly accepted defeat, and suffered less bombing, and destruction, and fewer deaths. All nations survived and rose again.

---

136 Gilbert, p 81

Many people agree that war is so terrible that it should be the last resort, after all other possibilities have been tried. But many politicians, in nations that they believe to be powerful, lose patience too quickly, and believing they can win, respond to popular nationalist sentiment and go to war too readily.

Conclusion

There were many alternatives for Britain in 1939-40 other than all-out war with Germany, depending on what objectives were to be pursued. Most involved the acceptance of the reality of German power, and influence, and trying to limit its worst effects, through meetings, discussion, international negotiation, the League of Nations, increasing understanding and goodwill, and the planning, threat or use of effective sanctions. Early in 1939, Britain had been prepared to agree to most of Hitler's demands regarding Poland, and negotiations were close to agreement. But Britain had issued the foolish Polish Guarantee, and provoked Hitler; Poland refused to accept Russian involvement in a guarantee, and Hitler joined forces with Russia to conquer Poland. Rescuing Poland was no longer a possibility. There were two main objectives that were then achievable: peace, reconciliation, and increased understanding; and rescuing the Jews – by persuasion, publicity, exposing the disgrace, and the facilitation of massive emigration.

Those two would have helped to make the world a better place – more humane, co-operative, peaceful, and civilised.

War made the world a worse place and established an unfortunate precedent and way of thinking which has been used to try to justify subsequent wars.

Chapter 6
Chamberlain's War (1939-40)

Germany invaded Poland on 1st September 1939. Although Chamberlain desperately wanted to avoid war, not least because Britain was unprepared for war, he could not resist pressure from Parliament, or sidestep the 'Polish guarantee', and he declared war on Germany two days later.

At 11.15 am on Sunday September 3rd, 1939, Chamberlain spoke on the radio to the British nation, and it is worth quoting in full:

This morning, the British Ambassador in Berlin handed the German Government a final Note, stating that, unless we heard from them by 11 o'clock that they were prepared at once to withdraw troops from Poland, a state of war would exist between us.

I have to tell you now that no such undertaking has been received, and consequently this country is at war with Germany.

You can imagine what a bitter blow it is to me that all my long struggle to win peace has failed. Yet I cannot imagine that there is anything more or anything different that I could have done that would have been more successful.

Up to the very last it would have been quite possible to have arranged a peaceful and honourable settlement between Germany and Poland, but Hitler would not have it. He had evidently made up his mind to attack Poland whatever happened, and although he now says he put forward reasonable proposals which were rejected by the Poles, that is not a true statement. The proposals were never shown to the Poles, nor to us, and although they were announced in a German broadcast on Thursday night, Hitler did not wait to hear comments on them, but ordered his troops to cross the Polish frontier. His action shows convincingly that there is no chance of expecting that this man will give up his practice of using force to gain his will. He can only be stopped by force.

We and France are today, in fulfilment of our obligations, going to the aid of Poland who is so bravely resisting this wicked and unprovoked attack on her people. We have a clear conscience. We have done all that any country could do to establish peace. The situation in which no word given by Germany's ruler could be trusted, and no people or country could feel themselves safe, has become intolerable. And now that we have resolved to finish it, I know that you will play your part with calmness and courage.

At such a moment as this, the assurances of support we have received from the Empire are a source of profound encouragement to us.

The Government have made plans under which it will be possible to carry on the work of the nation in the days of stress and strain that may be ahead. But these plans need your help. You may be taking your part in the fighting services or as a volunteer in one of the branches of Civil Defence. If so you will report for duty in accordance with the instructions you have received. You may be engaged in work essential to the prosecution of war for the maintenance of the life of the people – in factories, in transport, in public utility concerns, or in the supply of other necessaries of life. If so it is of vital importance that you should carry on with your jobs.

Now may God bless you all. May he defend the right. It is the evil things that we shall be fighting against – brute force, bad faith, injustice, oppression and persecution – and against them I am certain that right will prevail.

He presented the war as being 'right' versus evil. AJP Taylor[137] states that

---

137 A J P Taylor, *Origins, p 100*

In principle and in doctrine, Hitler was no more wicked and unscrupulous than many other contemporary statesmen.

That was presumably in their pursuit of their national interest.

If Western morality seemed superior, this was largely because it was the morality of the status quo. Hitler's was the morality of revision.

Conventional wisdom and morality in the West was that Germany should have continued to accept the status quo of the borders established in 1919. Germany' view was that it should take back what was previously German and had been illegitimately taken from it in 1919.

There is no doubt that Chamberlain had done his best to avoid war[138], and achieved enormous popularity for so doing. But this popularity was short-lived, and soon there was support for war, particularly in Parliament and the newspapers.

At first the war may not have been strictly necessary in accordance with the terms of the Polish guarantee. It did not guarantee particular borders, or guarantee against any kind of invasion. It guaranteed Polish independence. Clearly Hitler wanted the international city of Danzig (majority German), and improved access to the Polish Corridor to facilitate access to that part of Germany (East Prussia) which lay on the other side.

It was also premature. Hitler's peace proposals might not have been

---

138 Even a few days before Hitler invaded Poland the British were still trying to negotiate Peace with Germany. Hitler offered a pact with Britain once he had (re)occupied Poland. The British insisted that Hitler would have to desist from this aggression, and evacuate Czechoslovakia (Beevor, p 19)

shown to the British or to the Poles. But that was a mere technicality. They had been broadcast for all to hear. It seems that there was disagreement between the Poles and the British. The British were prepared to compromise over borders, over the status of Danzig, and over the Polish corridor. The Poles were not.

Chamberlain had the effrontery to say:

...no word given by Germany's ruler could be trusted.

But Britain's 'word' to come to the aid of Poland could not be trusted either. No Allied help was given to Poland when Germany invaded. Britain declared war, but effectively did nothing. The Polish Guarantee, given by Britain and France, should have applied equally to invasions from Russia or Germany. Russia invaded Poland 16 days after Hitler. But the Allies did not declare war on Russia, and Russia soon became an ally of Britain. It seems that Britain was mainly anti-German[139], could not be trusted, and cared little for Poland. Russia was free to invade wherever it liked[140], without 'interference' from Britain.

The 'aid' that Britain and France gave to Poland was that France invaded Saarland on the Western Front of Germany in the hope of helping Poland by drawing German troops from the East for defence to the West. The French offensive began on 7th September 1940. No German troops were withdrawn from the East. The offensive finished on 12th September 1940. In short, they did nothing that helped the Poles. Clearly, 'words' given by the British and French rulers could

---

139 The case for Britain to go to war with Russia was at least as strong. Hitler had grievances over Danzig, and over access to East Prussia through the Polish Corridor. The Russians had grievances over Western Ukraine (taken by Poland). Both were in breach of the Polish Guarantee

140 See the penultimate page of Chapter 3

not be trusted.

Hitler's 'words' had been clear all along (for example in Mein Kampf): he intended to invade Eastern Europe to gain more Lebensraum for Germany.

Britain's declaration of war on Germany did no good for Poland or the Jews – or for Britain.

At first it was a 'phoney war' with not much happening (compared with later), but the 'Battle of the Atlantic' began:

September 17th: the British aircraft carrier Courageous was sunk by a German submarine; 518 lives lost.

October 14th: the British battleship Royal Oak was sunk by a German submarine; 833 lives lost.

October 16th: Luftwaffe (German Air Force) attacked British ships in the Firth of Forth. The British fightback began with Spitfires shooting down German planes.

December 1939: Royal Navy attacked pocket battleship Admiral Graf Spee; it was scuttled and its tanker captured.

There was some air force activity on both sides, with reconnaissance flights, minor bombing raids and the RAF dropping propaganda leaflets over Germany (dubbed 'confetti war') but no desire for a major war or to 'die for Danzig'.

On September 17, 1939 the Soviets (in collusion with Germany) invaded Eastern Poland. Warsaw surrendered to the Germans on September 27, 1939.

The 'phoney war' ended when the invasion of France began (and coincidentally Churchill was appointed Prime Minister), on May 10, 1940. Churchill had been (as First Lord of the Admiralty) keen to start a proper war by stopping iron ore supplies to Germany from (neutral) Sweden.

In December 1939 Churchill was arguing, within the Government, for a campaign to stop those vital supplies of Swedish iron ore reaching Germany. In winter, much of the Baltic Sea was frozen and supplies were sent via Norway. Both countries were neutral. Churchill wanted to lay mines (in neutral waters) off Narvik. But the proposals were excessively discussed, much delayed, badly planned and co-ordinated, under-resourced, incompetently implemented and subject to constant change.

When finally, in April 1940, the Royal Navy was sent towards Norway, the Germans struck first. Fully aware of allied intentions, they occupied the major Norwegian ports before the British fleet arrived. Soon Norway was in Hitler's hands, and the world's greatest naval power had suffered a humiliating defeat

It was clear that Hitler had forewarning of the British invasion, and was determined to get there first. The Germans had received excellent intelligence on British intentions. Churchill's designs had been let loose by none other than himself. He dropped a series of hints in a secret conference with neutral press attachés in London on February 2 that had soon become known to German Intelligence.

It was almost as if Churchill wanted the Norway venture to go wrong.

Churchill was Chairman of the Military Co-ordinating Committee which had oversight of the Norway campaign

... but it is clear that his chairing [of the Committee] produced disorder

where there was already too much of it [141].

By April 24, 1940 Churchill was wanting greater control over the Committee. This placed Chamberlain in a dilemma. On the one hand he did not want to effectively give Churchill overall command of the war. Churchill's judgement was suspect and he sometimes behaved like 'a spoiled sulky child' [142]. On the other hand Chamberlain feared what Churchill might do if he opposed him.

Rumour had it that [Churchill] intended to "go down to the House of Commons and say that he could take no responsibility for what is happening" [143]. That would leave Chamberlain dangerously exposed. It would not do if his First Lord of the Admiralty were to wash his hands of the whole Norway business and leave Chamberlain to take the blame. That would lead to "a first class political crisis because the country believes that Winston is the man of action who is winning the war and little realise how ineffective, and indeed harmful, much of his energy is proving itself to be" [144].

For example, Churchill had changed his mind four times about the Trondheim (Norway) campaign.

Chamberlain found it difficult to retain Churchill's support, and his demands for more power, whilst at the same time controlling his worst excesses. Chamberlain even considered giving up his 'burden' (being Prime Minister). On May 1, Chamberlain announced that

---

141 Charmley, p 390. The disorder seemed typical of Churchill's personality. But we should not exclude the possibility that there was an element of political manipulation intended to attribute criticism and blame to Chamberlain, and to line himself up as a worthy successor as Prime Minister

142 Self, p 418; Charmley, p 390

143 Ponting, *Churchill*, p 427

144 Charmley, *Churchill*, p 390

Churchill, on behalf of the Military Co-ordinating Committee, was responsible for giving guidance and directions to the Chiefs of Staff.

The problems due to the Norway campaign had come to a head by May 1940, and in the House of Commons this led to a vote of confidence regarding Chamberlain. Although he won the vote it was with a much reduced majority, and this led to his resignation and to the appointment of Churchill as Prime Minister.

Obviously it was an important time for Churchill:

Having regained office when he was almost sixty-five, he knew that he had his last chance to become Prime Minister. He hoped to play the role of Lloyd George in WW1 and overthrow the Prime Minister if the war did not go well. He was therefore determined to take every opportunity to increase his personal standing ... [and] *he was determined to use the opportunity* [of becoming First Lord of the Admiralty] *to get to the top* [145].

Whilst still at the Admiralty he kept the right to announce all good news himself, and to create the impression that only the navy appeared to be taking much active part in the war. When there was a lack of good news, he was prepared to embroider it, or even make it up. For example on Nov 12, 1939 he announced that there had been an attack on German U-Boats, and they had paid a heavy toll. But only 6 out of 57 had been sunk. On 20 January 1940 he reassured his listeners that it seemed 'pretty certain' that the navy had sunk half the boats with which Germany began the war. In fact only 9 out of 57 had been sunk. His exaggerations continued; a few weeks later he said that the Germans had only had 12 U-Boats remaining, when it was really 40.

Churchill's misleading U-Boat campaign of lies and distortion served

---

145   Ponting, *Churchill*, p 412; and Ponting, *1940*, p 62

to enhance his reputation, and to put him in pole position to succeed if Chamberlain should fall, which he did after the Norway debate in Parliament.

In the early days of May 1940 there were rumours of a 'cabal' against Chamberlain and suggestions that Churchill, widely portrayed as a man of action and vigour, with the country behind him, should be Prime Minister. But Chamberlain's supporters underestimated Churchill's political skills, and considered the suggestion as little more than 'risible'. Churchill of course had to, and did, appear to be loyal to Chamberlain, but that did not stop his acolytes from creating mischief and encouraging opposition to Chamberlain.

The Norway debate was on Wednesday and Thursday May 7 and 8, 1940. Initially the Labour Party did not even intend to call a vote, but were persuaded to do so during the debate. Chamberlain opened the debate with a lacklustre speech. There was much criticism of the general conduct of the war, for which Chamberlain rather than Churchill was blamed. The Liberal Leader (Archibald Sinclair) was firmly anti-Chamberlain. Sir Roger Keys, splendidly dressed as an Admiral of the Fleet complete with gold braid and medals, said:

I have great admiration and appreciation for my right honourable friend the First Lord of the Admiralty. I am longing to see proper use made of his great abilities.

L S Amery, who Chamberlain thought would support him, used the famous words:

You have sat too long here for any good you have been doing. Depart, I say, and let us have done with you. In the name of God, go.

Although not originally intended as such the vote at the end of the debate turned into a vote of confidence in the government.

Lloyd George, not a friend of Chamberlain, said:

The nation is prepared for every sacrifice so long as it has leadership... I say solemnly that the Prime Minister should give an example of sacrifice because there is nothing that can contribute more to victory in this war more than that he should sacrifice the seals of office.

When it came to the vote, the government easily won with a majority of 81. But the normal government majority was 213. About 60 Conservative MPs had abstained. Chamberlain could not survive such a loss of confidence, and it was generally agreed that a Coalition Government was needed. Labour would not serve under Chamberlain. There was intensive activity over the next couple of days, and accounts differ.

Churchill was aware, before the debate, that he could be made the fall guy for the Norway debacle. The Whips were putting it about that it was all the fault of Winston who had made another forlorn failure. But Churchill was aware of this threat and was manoeuvring for his own future, keeping in close touch with members of the Labour and Liberal parties. These contacts were noticed by Channon who wrote in his diary (on 25th April):

Winston, it seems, has had secret conversations and meetings with Archie Sinclair [Liberal], A V Alexander [Labour] and Mr Attlee, and they are drawing up an alternative government.[146]

According to Roberts[147]

It was a sensational parliamentary coup preceded by massive behind-the-scenes intrigues and deals.

---

146 Ponting, *1940,* p 57
147 Roberts, p 88

Halifax was the preferred candidate of both the King and Chamberlain himself to succeed as Prime Minister. But he was not willing. Perhaps he felt he could not cope with a too-powerful Churchill in his government; perhaps he assumed that Churchill would fail, and he would succeed later. During these manoeuvrings Hitler started his invasion of France; and on the same day, Churchill was appointed Prime Minister on Chamberlain's recommendation.

There are a number of puzzling aspects to this:

1. Chamberlain easily won the vote of confidence, albeit with a reduced majority.
2. Chamberlain remained much more popular in the Conservative Party than Churchill was.
3. There was suddenly a perceived need for a Coalition Government, but Labour refused to serve under Chamberlain.
4. Chamberlain recommended to the King who should replace him, but considered only two candidates, Halifax and Churchill. Halifax refused to serve, which left only Churchill.
5. There were several other possible candidates. Sir Samuel Hoare had recently been Home Secretary and Foreign Secretary (under Baldwin) and was Lord Privy Seal in the War Cabinet (under Chamberlain). David Lloyd George was still considering the possibility that Churchill would fail, and he would be called upon to come to the country's rescue. There were also a number of leading Conservatives, including Halifax, who considered Churchill's appointment only temporary, and that he would fail, and that one of them would replace him.
6. The one minister who was responsible for the failed Norway campaign more than any other was Churchill himself. Yet he was the one to benefit.

There is perhaps no greater irony in the history of the Second World War that the Cabinet Minister who stood most exposed to criticism over the disaster of the Norwegian Expedition of April-May 1940 should have risen to supreme power on the back of it[148].

Churchill could certainly be an effective political manipulator (perhaps there is no other way of becoming Prime Minister). It is not clear what attempts were made to organise the Norway debate, but a very effective array of people emerged in that debate to attack Chamberlain. Churchill spoke well as a Chamberlain loyalist. Perhaps enough opposition to Chamberlain had already been organised, and he needed to gain the support of some Chamberlain loyalists.

Churchill had a small number of close followers who could manoeuvre for him. Probably, on his behalf, several had organised, or at least encouraged, a powerful display of opposition to Chamberlain, and turned the debate into a vote of confidence in Chamberlain. But they left few fingerprints. Many prefer to believe that Churchill was called to save the nation[149], rather than that he seized power in a ruthless political manoeuvre.

Although it is always possible to present a war as being some sort of moral crusade, there is no doubt that Churchill was keen to use whatever circumstances might allow to be in power and to be Prime Minister. His struggles to retain that position, dependent as it was on the continuation of the war, continued for another couple of years. He was far from having overwhelming support.

---

148 Howard, p 92
149 The desperate plight of Britain with the invasion of France, took place immediately AFTER Churchill had effectively seized power

Chapter 7
Churchill Takes Over

Churchill was appointed Prime Minister on May 10, 1940. This Chapter shows his determination to continue with the war. It examines the case for a negotiated peace in the early part of the war, with some illustrations of the continuing alleged movement for a negotiated peace, including examining some of the claims made for Hess's peace mission (a year later, May 10, 1941) and the Duke of Kent's mysterious death (August 25, 1942). Finally, it discusses why Churchill was determined to continue with the war.

In his book, The Second World War, Churchill wrote:

I felt as if I were walking with destiny, and that my past life had been but a preparation for this hour and this trial. I was sure I should not fail.

The day after his appointment he went to the House of Commons and made a short speech, including the well-known phrase 'I have nothing to offer but blood, toil, tears and sweat', concluding with the more dubious '… what is our aim? I can answer in one word. It is victory. Victory at all costs, victory in spite of all terror, victory however long and hard the road may be; for without victory there is no survival'.

At ALL costs?

NO survival?

Brilliant oratory, but unacceptable as policy.

All costs? Even if victory means 2 or 3% of the world's population being killed, Britain losing its Empire, becoming bankrupt, massively in debt to America, subservient to America, and most of Eastern Europe being dominated by the Soviet Communist regime? Very few members of the Government or of Parliament would have signed up for this, although Churchill himself might have done. He said (in opposing a negotiated peace):

*...We shall go on and we shall fight it out.... And if at last the long story is to end, it were better it should end, not through surrender, but only when we are **rolling senseless on the ground**.* [Emphasis added]

Probably most people would rather have survived, but perhaps Churchill was thinking more about his place in History, than about the lives and welfare of British (and other) people.

No Survival? That was true of many Jews and others (see Chapters 5 & 8). But it was not true of Germany, Denmark, or the Channel Islands, or many other places.

Surrender? Churchill seems to conflate the idea of 'negotiated peace' with 'surrender', presumably because most people would prefer the former to the latter; but Churchill did not want a negotiated peace. Yet they are two very different words, concepts and policies, and Churchill used his verbal skills to treat them as if they were the same.

The day after he was appointed, Churchill went to the House of Commons, together with Attlee (Labour Leader) his new Deputy, where he received a less than enthusiastic reception from Conservative MPs. Chamberlain had been given a 'terrific reception' (according to Nicolson). Chamberlain was still overwhelmingly popular. 'MPs lost their heads; they cheered; they waved their Order Papers and his reception was a regular ovation.'

Churchill was not well received. His thin cheers came almost exclusively from the Labour and Liberal benches. He said, as he left the Chamber:

I shan't last long[150].

Butler reckoned that more than three-quarters of Conservative MPs were ready to put Chamberlain back[151].

For at least two months after he took office Einzig recorded that Tory MPs would sit in 'sullen silence' when he rose to speak, even after he had completed one of his historic speeches. When the Labour benches cheered, the Tories were still plotting to get rid of him. On about 13 May William Spens, the chairman of the 1922 Committee of Tory backbenchers, said that three-quarters of his members were willing to give Churchill the heave-ho and put Chamberlain back.[152]

With regard to the task in hand, 'winning' the war, Churchill said:

I hope it is not too late. I am very much afraid it is. [153]

Moreover, Hitler had indicated that he wanted Peace with Britain. But Churchill, with limited support politically, was determined to carry on with the War.

Churchill changed two things almost immediately:

1. He arranged for the cabinet to authorise Allied bombing of German cities, the first being Monchengladbach, only days after he was appointed. Germany already had bombed civilian targets in Poland, in support of ground forces, and a bomber had lost its

---

150 Johnson, p 32
151 Howard, p 94
152 Johnson, p 32
153 Jenkins, p 592

way and 'accidentally' bombed over London. But serious German bombing of British cities did not begin for another three or four months.

Allied bombing of Germany killed about 500,000 people, injured 780,000, and rendered 7,500,000 homeless; 18 German cities were more than 50% destroyed.

German bombing of Britain killed about 60,000 people. Accounts of the dreadful suffering in Britain are widely available. There seem to be fewer accounts (at least in British Histories), of the massive suffering in Germany from Allied bombing which was about eight times worse. This indiscriminate killing is hard to defend.

2. Within two weeks of Churchill being appointed, Defence Regulation 18B was dramatically strengthened to give the Government virtually unlimited power of imprisonment without trial for opponents of the war. This was the 'freedom' for which Britain was fighting. It made it virtually impossible to judge the extent of opposition to the war; those who were not (yet) imprisoned had to be very careful what they said.

There were good reasons why Britain should not continue with the war in late May 1940:

• Almost everyone remembered the horror and slaughter of the First World War, and did not want another war like that. Almost every town and village had its own War Memorial, commemorating those who had fallen. Almost every family was affected by the death or injury (mental or physical) of someone close. After WW1 there was more than a decade of idealism. Many said they would never fight again. The League of Nations was founded to settle international disputes. There was almost universal acceptance of World Peace as an important objective, and even movements towards World Government, and discussions of the possibility of adopting the international language, Esperanto.

- Such idealism did not vanish overnight. A substantial body of opinion was opposed to continuing the war, and wanted a negotiated peace.

- Britain's position was hopeless militarily, and was becoming worse. Hitler had already annexed Austria and most of Czechoslovakia; the previous month he had begun his (successful) occupation of Denmark and Norway; the British Expeditionary Force had been cornered near Dunkirk, and there was no knowing how many, if any, would be rescued. On the day Churchill was appointed Hitler invaded Belgium, the Netherlands and Luxembourg. A month later Italy declared war on Britain and France; less than two weeks later France had surrendered.

Britain had no allies in Europe, and its navy, that 'ruled the waves', was of little relevance in most of the European war, and did not stop Hitler even in Norway.

Hitler's army was more than four times as big as Britain's (most of which could easily have been lost at Dunkirk). The chances of Britain defeating Hitler without substantial help from much bigger powers were approximately zero.

- Much of the Cabinet was opposed to continuing with the war, and Churchill's political manoeuvring to enable him to continue with the war are summarised below.

- Hitler offered peace, and had no quarrel with Britain. His ambitions lay in Central and Eastern Europe.

- Britain's position was also hopeless financially (See Chapter 8). The Government had borrowed and taxed heavily, but resources would not last, and senior ministers knew that Britain would not be able to fight a long war.

- For many, communism rather than Nazism, was the main enemy.

1. Cabinet opposition to war

The day after he was appointed Prime Minister, Churchill went to the House of Commons and announced his policy: victory at all costs. That was his policy personally; it had not been endorsed by the Cabinet.

Writing after the war, Churchill said:

... the supreme question of whether we should fight on alone never found a place on the War Cabinet agenda. It was taken for granted and as a matter of course by these men of all parties... and we were much too busy to waste time on such unreal, academic issues.

This 'mendacity' and 'misinformation' is a warning that we cannot take at face value the self-justifying words of participants after the event. Perhaps we should take all that Churchill wrote with a large pinch of salt.

On May 26, 27 and 28 there were nine cabinet meetings – remarkable in itself, and also a sign that Churchill was having trouble persuading the War Cabinet to adopt his policies (however much he might deny it subsequently).

At first there were only five members of the War Cabinet: Churchill, Chamberlain and Halifax (Conservative); and Attlee and Greenwood (Labour). Churchill could rely on the support of the two Labour members of his War Cabinet, but had difficulty with Chamberlain and Halifax. Part way through the intense series of meetings, Churchill co-opted Sinclair who was reliably anti-appeasement. The series of meetings was at the beginning of the Dunkirk Evacuations, and Churchill could easily argue for delaying decisions (as he did at the third Cabinet meeting (early evening, Sun May 26)) until the outcome of that evacuation was clear, or until he got his own way. It seemed that, initially, Chamberlain sat on the fence while Halifax argued determinedly for exploring the possibility of a negotiated peace; Churchill had to (appear to) make some concession to Halifax. He could hardly carry the Conservative Party with him if he could not convince Halifax.

On Monday 27 May there were again three Cabinet meetings. After the second (4.30pm) Halifax recorded:

I thought Winston talked the most frightful rot, also Greenwood, after bearing it for some time I said exactly what I thought of them, adding that if it really was their view, and if it came to the point, our ways must separate. But it does drive one to despair when he works himself up into a passion of emotion when he ought to make his brain think and reason.

Halifax argued against trying to fight on alone if France were defeated; he thought Britain's aim should be to preserve the country's integrity and independence, not to crush Germany. There was much discussion about asking Mussolini (still not on side with Hitler) to mediate, and whether the request should come from Britain (perhaps jointly with France) or from Roosevelt.

Churchill took Halifax for a walk in the garden where his charm, affection and powers of persuasion seemed to be effective. At the subsequent Cabinet meeting, Churchill's views were far from clear. He still wanted to fight on, alone if necessary, but he also had to favour peace negotiations to keep Halifax on board. Halifax asked Churchill whether, if he were satisfied that matters vital to the independence of this country were satisfied, he would be prepared to discuss terms. The Prime Minister replied that he would be thankful to get out of our present difficulties on such terms, provided we retain the essentials and elements of our vital strength, even at the cost of some territory. It is not clear what 'some territory' might have meant: probably the restoration of some British-controlled former German colonies, and perhaps territories such as Gibraltar or Malta as sweeteners to Italy. But at the same time as discussing the possibility of negotiation, Churchill also appeared to suggest that he would not contemplate any course other than fighting to the finish.

If Herr Hitler were prepared to make peace on the terms of the restoration of German colonies and the overlordship of Central Europe, that was one thing. But it was quite unlikely that he would make any such offer.

This was an assertion for which Churchill had no evidence. Indeed, those are the terms on which Hitler would most likely have settled. Hitler would not have ceded Czechoslovakia, Poland or Austria which, at times, Britain seemed to demand. But Hitler was less interested in Western Europe, and colonies, and there was plenty of room for negotiation.

Monday's cabinet meetings terminated with the main issue unresolved. Discussions continued at the second meeting the following day. Halifax argued that Britain might get better terms before France went out of the war than after. Churchill argued that if Hitler got Britain to the Conference Table, the terms then offered would affect Britain's independence and integrity. Thus there were two opinions, with no real evidence to support them, and continuing disagreement. Churchill made other dubious assertions (which may have sounded good and been effective at the time):

• Nations that went down fighting rose again, but those which surrendered were finished;

- The chance of decent terms being offered to Britain were a thousand to one against.
- Churchill could achieve a majority in the War Cabinet, especially with the addition of Sinclair. But that was not enough. He needed unanimity, and could not afford to lose his Foreign Secretary, and perhaps Chamberlain too. If those two left, he could easily lose most of the Conservative Party, his majority in Parliament, and his Premiership.
- He then called a much larger meeting of all ministers of Cabinet rank (Halifax was absent), and made some more dubious assertions:
- It is idle to think that if we tried to make peace now we should get better terms from Germany than if we went on and fought it out.
- We should become a slave state with a German puppet government.

At the following War Cabinet meeting (the ninth in three days) he told them that the other ministers

Had expressed the greatest satisfaction when he had told them that there was no chance of our giving up the struggle. He did not remember ever before having heard a gathering of persons occupying high places in political life, express themselves so emphatically.

His speech was genuinely popular with other ministers; many may have thought that they were merely endorsing the position adopted by the War Cabinet. They were not. Churchill had manoeuvred with great skill to gain support for continuing the war.

Halifax began retreating from his position, and Chamberlain was worn down too. Churchill's warmongering had won the day, and it became official policy not to seek peace, and to pursue war 'at all costs'.

Chamberlain came around to support Churchill's point of view, but died of cancer six months after Churchill became Prime Minister. In December 1940, the British Ambassador in America died; it was an opportunity for Churchill to get rid of his enemies. He tried to persuade Lloyd George to go, but the wily Welsh wizard would not. Instead Halifax was despatched to Washington DC. Hoare, the most senior member of Chamberlain's government to be excluded from Churchill's Government, was soon despatched to Spain as Ambassador. The Duke of Windsor, suspected of being pro-Nazi, was made Governor of the Bahamas on August 18, 1940, and sent out of the way. His brother, the Duke of Kent, was killed in a secret and mysterious flying accident on 25th August 1942, apparently still active in some sort of international discussions.

2. Hitler offered Peace

Immediately after Churchill became Prime Minister, Hitler was at the peak of his power and reputation. It looked as though France would fall, and Hitler had already over-run the Rhineland, Austria, Czechoslovakia, Poland, Belgium, the Netherlands, Luxembourg, Denmark and Norway. It also looked as if most of the British Expeditionary Force would be lost (Churchill could not at this time know how successful the evacuation of Dunkirk would be). But Britain's position could become still worse which is why Halifax argued for getting the best terms they could in late May 1940. Perhaps the BEF would be lost, and Britain could then have been invaded.

Hitler made it clear on July 19, 1940 that he was willing to discuss peace with Britain. He did not give detailed proposals but the main features of the terms of peace to which Hitler would have agreed are fairly clear; there was also some wriggle room. Hitler was willing to agree to leave Britain and its Empire alone, perhaps even to help them. He might have been willing to withdraw from Western Europe. He was not willing to withdraw from Central and Eastern Europe, where he wanted some sort of overlordship, and lebensraum. Most of all he wanted to be left to fight Russia without British interference. Britain might have been willing to offer a few sweeteners, such as former German Colonies which Britain controlled, or Malta or Gibraltar.

Churchill wanted to ensure the independence of Britain, and succeeded in persuading Britain that it was under threat. He even suggested that Germany might demand the British navy, although there was no evidence for this. Britain would have come to an accommodation with Germany over the Polish Corridor, and Danzig; but the Poles were intransigent. Britain would have liked Hitler to withdraw from Czechoslovakia and Poland, but he would not.

Churchill may have been thinking that the war effort would soon exhaust Germany, and that Hitler and his regime would soon implode. But it was Britain that could not sustain the war effort and was bankrupt a year or so later, sending begging letters to America. Thus Britain's position in 1941 was weaker and the delay and war (1940-41) achieved nothing. Churchill thought

The Americans were preparing themselves for a total collapse of the British position in the Mediterranean.

The same day he spoke to his close advisers about the possibility of such a collapse in the Middle East and of having to make a compromise peace. On 4th May 1941 he wrote to Roosevelt referring to the possible loss of Egypt and the Middle East ...

And a long and extremely difficult oceanic war ... with most of Africa and Asia dominated by Germany, and he asked America to declare war.

Roosevelt did not even reply.

Churchill gambled everything on America joining the war against the Nazis. Eventually they did so, but it was very much in their own interests: further boosting the American armaments industry, and also gaining increasing influence over the British Empire as Britain's finances declined. Roosevelt told one member of his Cabinet:

We have been milking the British financial cow, which had plenty of milk at one time but which has now about become dry[154]

In some ways they were like vultures grabbing what they could after Churchill's war had drained the blood out of a rotting corpse.

First there was the destroyers-for-bases deal. Britain handed over bases in Trinidad, Bermuda and Newfoundland in return for fifty mothballed destroyers[155].

Then there was the Lend-Lease arrangement which Churchill defended in public as the most unsordid act in history. But

In private he said that Britain was being skinned and flayed to the bone[156].

Churchill's position as prime minister was at first weak, dependent as he was on the reluctant support of the Conservative Party, and on Chamberlain and Halifax. In the summer of 1940, foreign newspapers publicised rumours[157] that the Duke of Windsor was about to be asked to negotiate peace, and was working with Lloyd George. It was certainly credible that Windsor would have been willing to negotiate peace.

---

154 Charmley, *Churchill,* p 433
155 Johnson, p 251
156 Johnson, p 252
157 Detailed in Cadbury, p 180

3. Peace Party

There was never formally a peace party in Britain, although there was a good deal of anti-war feeling especially in the 1920s and early 1930s, and Hitler believed that there was a significant peace party in Britain with whom he could negotiate, if Churchill could be deposed. It is not possible to say how much opposition to the war there was, nor is it clear how long it lasted.

Both Hitler and his deputy, Hess, believed that there was a peace party in Britain, and that the war was promoted only by Churchill and his clique. It seems unlikely that in the early years of the war they were both mad and both very badly-informed, and even Churchill feared a 'peace party'.

He knew that Roosevelt was aware that the peace movement was a reality – he had been told as much by his officials in London. In December 1940 the US Military Attaché had reported to the President that the City was 'ready for appeasement at any time'.[158]

But Churchill needed military supplies from America and could not afford to be seen as considering a negotiated settlement. And American industry needed the orders from Britain for Churchill's war.

In general terms, until the mid-1930s, the majority of the population was very anti-war – after the horrors of the First World War.

The famous Oxford Union debate, in which a majority of 275 : 153 declared that they would in no circumstances fight for its King and Country, took place in 1933. This was not an unusual expression of sentiment. A similar motion had been passed at Cambridge six years previously.

---

158 Picknett et al, *Hess cover up*, p 320

Organisations like the Peace Pledge Union[159] were at their height.

A Peace Ballot was conducted by a non-government organisation for the League of Nations in 1934-5. Five questions were asked by volunteers going door-to-door, and 11.6 million responded, which was 38% of the adult population. An overwhelming majority (around 90%) agreed that

- *Britain should be a member of the League of Nations*

This indicated some of the idealism of the period.

- *There should be an all-round reduction in armaments by international agreement*

Some blame was attached to the armaments manufacturers for the occurrence of wars. This was in line with the disarmament provisions which had been agreed at the end of WW1, enforced on Germany, otherwise largely disregarded.

- *There should be an all-round abolition of national military aircraft by international agreement*

It seemed that there was general revulsion about bombing, which inevitably did substantial damage and killed and injured innocent victims. Governments too easily resort to bombing, which is easier than fighting on the ground with troops – especially for nations that want to cause fear, but haven't the will or resources to fight.

- *The manufacture and sale of armaments for private profit should be prohibited by international agreement*

---

159   100,000 members in 1936

The fifth question was concerned with whether there should be international action if one nation attacked another. The use of economic and other non-military measures was approved by 94%; the use of force was opposed by 25.7%.

There was overwhelming support for Chamberlain when he returned from Munich promising peace in our time. But this support did not last long.

By the late 1930s a good deal of opinion was shifting in favour of war because

1. There was increasing evidence of Nazi brutality and anti-Semitism. Those who favoured war seemed to go along with the strange moral stance that, as Hitler and leading Nazis were clearly 'baddies', the best thing to do was to shoot and bomb all Germans, destroy their homes and cities, and kill as many as possible[160]. Or perhaps they believed that there could be war without deaths and destruction. Pacifists are often accused of being naïve. But those who advocate wars seem to have little idea of the realities of war.
2. Hitler had breached the Munich agreement, taken all of Czechoslovakia, and treated the British Prime Minister with contempt.
3. Britain had declared war on Germany, and people tended to rally around the flag and respond to the call of duty.
4. Some, encouraged by the newspapers and the media, had exaggerated ideas of Hitler's ambitions – he was going to conquer all of the world and destroy Christian civilisation, freedom and

---

160 Perhaps it was comparable with King Herod's idea: He wanted to kill all male children to be sure of getting Jesus. But he failed. As did Churchill and WW2; only Hitler managed to kill Hitler; and no-one saved six million Jews

democracy. Certainly Churchill's rhetoric, for example with references to 'this monstrous regime', was effective (except in Germany, the Low Countries, Scandinavia and much of Europe).

In 1939-40 the war seemed to be pursued in rather a half-hearted way – it was known as the 'phoney war'. Then Churchill took over, and was determined to eliminate any signs of a 'Peace Party'.

Many, perhaps most, of the Royal Family and the aristocracy were at first opposed to the war. They saw the Soviets rather than Germany being the main enemy, especially after the murder of the Russian Royal Family, and were opposed to communism. Germany and Britain had a lot in common, and the achievements of the Nazis were widely admired (solving the unemployment problem, rising living standards, massive infrastructure projects such as autobahns and railways, restoring national pride). It was argued that Britain should keep out of any conflict in Central /Eastern Europe, where Britain had no important interests, and leave it to Germany and Russia to fight it out between themselves, and exhaust each other. There was some criticism of German anti-Semitism; but anti-Semitism was widespread, even in Britain, and some nations were as bad as Germany. But the Jews were hardly an issue in the early stages of the war, and the worst excesses of the Holocaust had not yet begun.

In 1936 King Edward VIII had been forced to abdicate, and he has taken much of the blame (or credit) for preferring a peaceful settlement, and also for apparently being pro-Nazi. He did not want to continue the war with Germany. Some key members of the Royal Family were in favour of a negotiated peace, including Edward VIII / Duke of Windsor and some of his brothers, especially the Duke of Kent, but they were not free to talk openly. Leading royals were also subject to military discipline. Churchill reminded the Duke of Windsor of this:

Your Royal Highness has taken active military rank, and refusal to obey direct orders of competent military authority will create a serious military situation. I hope it will not be necessary for such orders to be sent.

The same, of course, applied to his younger brothers, and it seems likely that he was not the only member of the Royal Family who still preferred Peace to War, even in 1940-1, and perhaps later. Of course the Duke exercised diplomatic duplicity, according to Morton[161]. In public he was circumspect about the war: he and his wife went out of their way to show their belief in final victory. In private it was a different story; he was defeatist. He believed that Britain faced a catastrophic military defeat which could only be avoided through a peace settlement.

The Duke of Windsor, and particularly his wife, were widely suspected of having Nazi sympathies, and were playing with fire. He was despatched to become governor of the Bahamas to get him away from Europe – where he was either too pro-German, or he was being taken advantage of to be used by Hitler as puppet king should Hitler conquer Britain. After the war had begun, when in Lisbon en route to the Bahamas, Windsor said:

...if he had remained on the throne, war would have been avoided.[162]

Before he became King Edward VIII, David (Prince Edward, later Duke of Windsor) was certainly very close to his younger brother, Prince George, Duke of Kent. With his wife, Kent kept up social visiting with their relatives in Austria, and it is possible to construe relationships with the Nazis, eg through their cousin, Prince Philipp of Hesse, who had risen to high ranks in the Nazi leadership.

---

161 Morton, p 168
162 Picknett et al, *Windsors,* p 164

The Duke and Duchess of Windsor (unofficially) visited Germany (October, 1937) as guests of the Nazis and received a 'royal' reception. It was clear that they did not want war with Germany. They met Goebbels who was delighted with the Duke; they discussed a thousand things, and Goebbels stated that, with him, an alliance would have been possible, declaring it a terrible shame[163].

A visit to America[164] was planned by Charles Bedaux who presented the ex-king as Head of the Peace Movement.

While King George VI and Queen Elizabeth were visiting America (May 1939) the Duke of Windsor seemed to be trying to upstage them with a speech on NBC America which was an evocative plea for world peace:

... as a soldier of the last war...praying that such cruel and destructive madness shall never again overtake mankind.[165]

In 1940 he said:

*The most important thing now to be done was to end the war before thousands more were killed or maimed **to save the faces of a few politicians.***

Today that seems a mild and humane enough thing to say, and it is interesting the way he saw the role of politicians. Weddell, the American Ambassador in Spain, pointed out to the American Secretary of State that these views

...represented an element in England, possibly a growing one who

---

163 Goebbels' Diary as cited in Gerwin Strobl, *The Germanic Isle*, p 109-10
164 It was planned, but cancelled
165 Cadbury, p 84

supported Windsor and *who hope to come into their own in the event of peace.*[166]

In December 1940 the Duke was reported as saying:

... it would be a tragic thing for the world if Hitler were to be overthrown. Hitler is the right and logical leader of the German people... Hitler is a very great man.[167]

Windsor always bore in mind the possibility of his returning to Britain and taking over as King (with Wallis as Queen). He was aware that he had to obey orders from the government, but when the time was right, he was prepared to return from the Bahamas immediately, and he agreed a code word that would trigger his immediate return[168]. Some, who were confident of a German victory, predicted that Windsor would become the First President of the Great British Republic[169].

Speaking in favour of peace before the war had begun was (just, or nearly) acceptable. But it became clear that Churchill had to suppress all talk of peace[170] if he was to persuade the Americans to join him in the war, and suggests that there was a real threat to his position from the ex-king and those who wanted a negotiated peace.

He ordered the foreign secretary to ensure that all public officials were strictly forbidden to talk of peace[171].

---

166 Cadbury, p 164
167 Morton, p 213
168 Morton, p 193
169 Morton, p 178
170 Or negotiations or surrender or defeat; Churchill managed to conflate these words
171 Churchill, *Second World War,* Vol 2, p 152

Walter Scott, the 8th Duke of Buccleuch, and brother-in-law of the Duke of Gloucester, held high office as the King's Lord Steward and made no secret of his pro-German views. He had to be talked to and got rid of. But there were also suspicions about his successor, the Duke of Hamilton. Shortly after the invasion of Poland Hamilton wrote to *The Times*[172] pointing to the injustices that had been done to the German people in the past, that once the threat of aggression was removed, war was 'wrong and meaningless'.

It was, however, difficult for people to express their views openly because of Defence Regulation 18B which had first been introduced in 1939 to allow the internment of Nazi sympathisers. Within a fortnight of Churchill becoming Prime Minister the regulation was toughened to allow widespread detentions of those thought to be on the far right. Oswald Mosley was immediately arrested, and by the end of the year there were more than a thousand detainees. The Regulation gave wide powers for detention without trial, and meant that anyone who preferred a negotiated peace had to be very careful what they said, and who they associated with.

In July 1940 Churchill put in hand a campaign against unhelpful rumours, including the advice 'If you know anybody who makes a habit of causing worry and anxiety by passing on rumour and who says things persistently that might help the enemy – tell the police, but only as a last resort'.

One case led to a month in jail for a man who said that Britain had no chance of winning the war[173]. Sometimes ordinary people were arrested for doing no more than complain about the prices in bread queues[174].

---

172 October 1939
173 Ponting, *Churchill,* p 459
174 Roberts, p 122

Thus it was difficult to express views in favour of peace and negotiation.

There were no avenues in Britain in late 1940 short of mass demonstrations in the streets through which views could be made known in the media or in politics. As Churchill admitted earlier in the year 'In time of war the machinery of government is so strong it can afford largely to ignore popular feeling'. The rumours circulating in the Midlands, as reported by Mass Observations, show how bad the situation seemed to many people and what could be believed. It was rumoured that train-loads of corpses had left Liverpool for mass burial, that martial law had been declared in a number of big cities, that food riots had broken out and that homeless and bombed people were on hunger marches with white flags[175] .

At first many of the aristocracy were opposed to the war against Germany.

Those were the days when Tory Prime Ministers had to pay more attention to the views of dukes and earls.

The Lords was full of ... surrender monkeys, arch-appeasers such as Lord Brocket, the Earl of Londonderry, Lord Ponsonby, the Earl of Danby, as well as Bendor, the Duke of Westminster, a flamboyant and charming personality who said that 'the war was part of a Jewish and Masonic plot[176]'.

Less than two weeks into the war, the Duke of Westminster held a pro-peace meeting at his home, Bourdon House, Mayfair. He was joined by many leading peers, including the Marquis of Tavistock, the Duke of Buccleuch, and Lord Noel-Buxton[177].

175 Ponting, *1940,* p 171
176 Johnson, p 230
177 Brother of Lord Rothermere who ran the *Daily Mail*

Lord Halifax, the Foreign Secretary, was in favour of peace negotiations in May 1940. His under-Secretary RAB Butler, who represented him in the House of Commons, was also labelled as an 'appeaser'. So also was RAB's Private Parliamentary Secretary, Sir Henry 'Chips' Channon, who in turn lived next door to the Duke of Kent, and was a friend of Mrs Simpson (who married ex-king Edward VIII). According to Howard[178], in 1938, RAB was

... soon to be pursued by various assorted noblemen pressing upon him the necessity of reaching an accommodation with Hitler, virtually at any price.

The Leader of the Labour Opposition, George Lansbury, had resigned because he objected to war.

Some of the best known people who preferred peace, supported the war eventually, for example Bertrand Russell, E M Forster, Leonard Woolf, David Garnett, Storm Jameson and Albert Einstein. But there was a period, approximately 1940-42, when it was unclear who still wanted a negotiated peace. There were still notable pacifists, including Vera Brittain, Sybil Thorndike and Aldous Huxley; and there were also many more conscientious objectors in WW2 than WW1.[179]

Some authors seem to delight in listing important people who seemed guilty by association with others who (had) wanted peace. Picknett et al[180] succeeded in listing all sorts of connections between royalty, aristocrats, politicians, and Nazis, and suggest that even social and family meetings between many of these characters were some sort of peace negotiations. It is clear that the Duke of Kent was well-informed and was probably an adviser to, and a conduit between

---

178 Howard, p 76
179 60,000 rather than 16,000
180 Picknett et al, *Hess*

British Kings[181] and the Germans; but that was before the war.

The Duke of Kent was considerably more than the leader of the Anglo-German peace group. He also took part in last-minute moves to avert the coming conflict, visiting his cousin Prince Philip of Hesse[182]... In July 1939 he initiated a plan in which he would negotiate directly ... [but] it is now impossible to find any details of it[183].

After war broke out, he had to be careful what he said and did, particularly in the light of Regulation 18B.

There was still significant support for peace, but Churchill could not brook such opposition. The strengthened Defence Regulation 18B was not much used against aristocrats, and most peace-lovers. But the threat was there, and many chose to keep quiet. The King observed in his diary:

These powers are so wide and sweeping that The Government have the power to control every person ... in this country.

Churchill and his war had survived politically and his reputation was enhanced – his popularity reaching 78%. But there were still threats to his political position, dependent as it was on the continuation of the war. After the fall of Tobruk (June 1942) his popularity fell to 41%. The main parties had agreed not to contest by-elections during the war, but independents could stand and the government

---

181 His father George V and his older brothers, Edward VIII and George VI
182 Prince Philip of Hesse was a Nazi, but fell out with them and was imprisoned in a concentration camp; he was a great grandson of Queen Victoria, distantly related to the Prince Philip who was a great great grandson of Queen Victoria, and became Queen Elizabeth II's husband. The Duke of Kent visited him for top level discussions early in 1939, before the war
183 Picknett et al, *Hess,* p 279

suffered a series of by-election defeats, most notably at Maldon. The possibility of getting rid of Churchill was discussed. Stafford Cripps sounded out opinion on whether he might succeed. There was a vote of confidence in the government; those opposed to the government included speakers with some daft[184] ideas, and the government won easily, but 25 MPs voted against, and another 27 abstained[185].

The extent of opposition to the Government and the War was not clear, but it was greater than subsequent (Churchill inspired) mythology suggests[186].

After the war Churchill was determined to maintain the heroic myths. He wrote in his war memoirs:

Future generations may deem it noteworthy that the supreme question of whether we should fight on alone never found a place upon the War Cabinet agenda ... we were much too busy to waste time on such unreal, academic issues.

Churchill was certainly economical with the truth.

It seems that at least as late as June 1940 Britain was still putting out peace feelers via Sweden and Italy, although it was hushed up[187].

4. Rudolf Hess Peace Mission

On 10th May 1941 Rudolf Hess, Hitler's deputy, flew to Britain to

---

184 One suggested that the King's brother, the Duke of Gloucester, should relieve Churchill of his military responsibilities; another suggested that Churchill should be given dictatorial powers
185 Ponting, *Churchill*, p 565
186 Ponting, *1940, p 103*
187 Ponting, *1940*, p113 provides details of relevant evidence

try and secure a settlement before Germany attacked the Soviet Union. The terms were probably much the same as Hitler would have offered in 1940 – the continuance of the British Empire in return for accepting German domination of central and eastern Europe.

During the previous year most of the British Expeditionary Force (but not its equipment) had been rescued. Otherwise Britain's position had not improved, and a year's fighting had not improved the possible peace terms. Britain might have been better, and certainly no worse, pursuing Halifax's preference of an approach to Mussolini to mediate. At the time Mussolini was still neutral, and by offering a few 'bribes' (eg the Suez, Malta, Gibraltar), might have been persuaded to intercede, and to stay neutral. Instead, he became another powerful enemy, and there was no peace.

The Hess mission is still shrouded in mystery with undisclosed and incomplete documents, secrecy, lies, bluff and double agents speaking with forked tongues. We do not know whether Hitler instructed Hess to make the trip, or whether it was done with Hitler's knowledge and approval, or totally at Hess's own initiative without Hitler knowing or approving. We do know that if things went wrong (and they did), arrangements were made that Hitler could deny all knowledge of it (and he did).

The Blitz concluded with a bad attack on London[188] on the very day of Hess's flight to Britain. It could have been coincidence that Hitler decided to move his air force attacks to the East (Russia). It is also likely that May 10 bombing was intended to show London what continued war could mean, and then the bombing was stopped to show the advantages of peace. There is a strong suspicion that Hitler knew about Hess's mission, and adjusted German bombing of

---

188   There was only sporadic bombing of Britain thereafter until the V1 and V2 bombs in 1944

Britain accordingly[189].

We do not know if the trip was at the invitation of Churchill (probably not), whether as part of a genuine quest for peace, or for entrapment to try to gain secret information; or whether it was at the invitation of a peace movement distinct from Churchill, but hoping to persuade Churchill; or whether it was at the invitation of Churchill's enemies (possibly including leading members of the Royal Family) – a supposed anti-Churchill clique who wanted to replace Churchill with someone (such as Lloyd George, or Hoare) who would negotiate peace. If this latter were the case, it is possible or even likely that Churchill knew what was going on, and managed to control events.

It seems likely that there was some pre-planned co-operation by the British to enable his plane to penetrate British defences and arrive near Glasgow.

It seems that Hess brought a major document, probably a draft peace treaty, although it has never been made public. Hess assumed that he could negotiate a peace agreement (initially with the King and/or the Duke of Hamilton (near whose house he landed), which suggests either that there had been previous negotiations[190], or, the conventional story, that Hess was seriously misinformed.

It suited both Hitler and Churchill to deny all knowledge of the trip (and of the Treaty). Hitler was about to invade Russia (he invaded on June 22), and wanted to take Russia by surprise (he did!). He did not want the Russians to think he was negotiating peace in the West to leave him free in the East to attack Russia. He wanted the

---

189   It is just possible that Hitler happened to transfer the bulk of the Luftwaffe to the East on the very day that Hess landed in Scotland
190   Hess had assumed that he could fly back to Germany after a few days; that would have required considerable help from the British

Russians to think that Germany was tied up in a war with Britain, and was planning to invade, thus leaving the Russians safe. If he had openly declared that Hess was negotiating peace with Britain so that he would be free to invade Russia, the surprise element would have been lost.

Similarly, Churchill did not want to be seen to be negotiating with Germany. He was busy trying to persuade the Americans to enter the war against the Nazis. He could not be seen to be contemplating peace with Germany, especially if Hitler was seen to be offering terms which made the war hardly worth continuing with. The more he could present the Nazis as warmongers who did not want peace, and wanted to invade more and more of the world, then the more they could be seen as a threat even to America.

Hess said[191] that America would be furious if Britain were to make peace now since she wanted to inherit the British Empire[192]; the longer the war lasts, the more the power relation between England and America becomes weighted in favour of the latter[193]. He was right about that. He gave a prophetic warning about the Soviet threat: a victory for England would equally be a victory for the Bolsheviks who would sooner or later march into Germany and the rest of Europe. Their military strength would surprise the rest of the world; but Soviet Russia was only at the beginning of her industrial development. Hess argued that Germany was going to win the war, and that England should ally with Germany against Russia. But even if Britain were to win the war, there was the danger of a Soviet takeover. He seemed to talk sense, and was not as mad as others subsequently implied.

---

191 In May 1941, Padfield, p 220
192 America wanted to inherit the British Empire; Hitler wanted to leave it alone
193 Padfield, p 267

It suited both Churchill and Hitler to say that Hess was simply mad[194]. It was Hess himself who had suggested to Hitler that if his mission went wrong, Hitler should say that Hess had gone mad.

Hess assumed that he would be welcomed by a peace party in Britain, including the Duke of Hamilton, who would take him to the King. He also seems to have assumed that the King could sack Churchill, and then appoint someone more amenable so that his peace treaty could be negotiated and adopted. He had, or claimed to have, a connection with the Duke of Hamilton, and with the King, having met his older brother on Sept 29, 1937 when the Duke (a fluent German speaker) and Duchess of Windsor were (controversially, perhaps provocatively) visiting Germany. On that occasion Goebbels is recorded as saying:

The duke is proud of his German blood. Says he is more German than he is British. There is no need to lose a single German life in invading Britain. The Duke and his wife will deliver the goods[195].

Presumably 'the goods' were peace with Britain, or perhaps joining Germany in an alliance against Russia.

Hess thought that the war was supported only by Churchill and his clique, and that Britain was bound to be defeated; and he wanted to stop the deaths and suffering. Germany's U-Boats would lead to starvation in Britain, bombing would undermine morale; the productive capacity of the enlarged Germany could far outstrip Britain's. Moreover, there must have been something very persuasive in his peace treaty, such that a blanket of secrecy has been thrown over it ever since.

Before the war, King George VI was pro-German, anti-Russian, pro-

---

194 To Churchill he was both mad and bad – he was after all a Nazi
195 Higham, p 251

Peace and anti-War, and hostile to Churchill. During the war he seemed to become the opposite, in line with his government. He was a constitutional monarch, reluctant to try to assert powers that he did not have (unlike Edward VIII), and Churchill was wily enough to keep him on board. Otherwise Churchill had powers to keep him quiet. A government had already disposed of one king, in 1936; George VI was not strong enough to stand against a government.

It is too simplistic to dismiss Hess as being mad and bad. He was a complex character, even if what he was trying to do, with hindsight, appears to be misguided. But if he had succeeded, our assessment of him would be very different. History tends to be the account of the winners – one of which Hess clearly was not.

Hess had continuing health problems, and carried a variety of homeopathic remedies, which may have seemed eccentric. His long imprisonment in Britain (then Spandau) affected him adversely, and he constantly feared being poisoned. He had mood swings and was sometimes depressed. It seems likely that he was given mind-altering drugs to encourage him to tell the truth, and to disclose German secrets. He seems to have had unrealistic expectations about the reception he would get in Britain. He once threw himself off a landing as if attempting suicide. He never seemed to give a full and frank account of himself and his mission (if he did, it has been hushed up). He appeared to be totally loyal to Hitler, and a believer in what Hitler was doing. At times he feigned memory loss (and perhaps other symptoms). But none of this meant he was mad. Someone who was clinically insane would not have survived seventeen years as Hitler's closest supporter, friend and collaborator, and for seven years as his Deputy. When he chose, he could, and did, write long, carefully argued reports even when imprisoned; many who met him considered him perfectly sane and rational.

He was, however, a torn and tortured man. On the one hand he was very close to Hitler and a great admirer of him; he supported him, loved[196] him, almost worshipped him and was totally loyal and devoted to him. He was the only one who could address Hitler with the familiar 'du' rather than the more formal 'Sie'. They were so close and complementary that they were almost like two sides of one person. Hess was the softer, more gentle side – which was largely absent in Hitler himself[197]. On the other hand, he was beginning to see the harder, crueller side of Hitler, and of Nazi atrocities. In his formal position, he received complaints about such abuses. Hess found this side of Hitler increasingly difficult to accept.

Dr H V Dicks[198] conducted a thorough study of the personality of Hess and others who held strong Nazi beliefs. He detected a strong correlation between fanaticism and the willing acceptance of a strong father during childhood. Hess had a repressed hatred of his father. His father was replaced by a repressed fantasy relationship with Hitler. He was tormented when realising the crueller side of Hitler. Perhaps he chose an alternative 'good father' in the Duke of Hamilton, representing the King, instead of the tarnished Hitler.

The infamous Kristallnacht (November 1938) had a profound effect on him. His friends told of his despair at the nationwide pogrom, that he was depressed as never before, and he (unsuccessfully) beseeched Hitler to stop the outrages. He suffered bouts of illness and sleeplessness[199]. The systematic massacre of European Jewry weighed heavily on Hess's mind, and he repeatedly expressed remorse[200].

---

196 There is no suggestion of a homosexual relationship
197 Although he was kind to his dog Blondi!
198 See McGinty, p 317-9
199 Padfield, p 48
200 Padfield, p 349

Later, at the Nuremberg Trials Hess said of Hitler:

I suppose every genius has a demon in him – you can't blame him – it's just him.[201]

Before his flight to Britain, Hess was becoming aware of the more extreme Nazi ideas for the extermination of the Jews. Although he was anti-Semitic, he did not like the idea of mass murder; he would have preferred to send the Jews abroad (eg to Palestine[202] and Madagascar). Hess, with his particularly close relationship with Hitler, was probably the only one who had any chance of (perhaps partially) diverting the Nazis from extermination to deportation. By imprisoning Hess, rather than negotiating with him, Churchill may have[203] deprived millions of Jews of their last chance to live.

Either Hess was very cautious about who he talked to and gave details of his peace proposals to, or the Government was very careful to hush up the details. Probably both. Loftus, a young officer who was posted to Mytchett Place to keep an eye on Hess, was sworn to secrecy. He signed a statement saying that nothing, either written or spoken, which had passed between himself and Hess has been or ever will be mentioned to anyone other than his commanding officer, Major Foley. But MI5 documents reveal that de Courcy was

---

201 McGinty, p 320
202 The British controlled Palestine, but placed a limit on the number of Jews it would allow. The British briefly considered setting up Jewish homelands in British Guiana and Western Australia (Padfield, p 47)
203 Unwittingly. Churchill could have said to a train-full of Jews on their way to the gas chambers, "Don't worry, I'm going to put a stop to all this, if I can get the Americans and the Russians to help me to win my war. It may take a few years and Britain has no money to help, and a few more million of you will have to be killed in the meantime. But it's a price worth paying. It will be worth it in the end." Of course Churchill did not say this, but that is what his policy amounted to

briefed on Hess's peace proposals, perhaps by Loftus's friend W S Pilcher, who was suddenly removed from his post and forced into professional and social exile.

Writing after the war, de Courcy gave details of the proposals, which were mostly in line with expectations, but in addition added most importantly and surprisingly:

The Jews would be deported to Palestine[204].

Such a proposal would not have suited Britain which controlled Palestine, and had already severely restricted the number of Jewish migrants.

If that really was part of the Peace Treaty it would explain why Britain and America had to keep the proposed peace treaty quiet at all costs. Even today it would still need to be kept secret. Roosevelt and Churchill would never have dared let it be known that they had refused a peace treaty that could have saved the lives of millions of Jews.

Both Hess and the Duke of Windsor[205] preferred mass emigration to wholesale slaughter[206].

Whatever a treaty proposed, there was always the possibility that Hitler would not deliver. But it was surely worth pursuing the possibility of saving millions of lives.

---

204 Padfield, p 346
205 A possible alternative Head of State in Britain – a possibility that Hitler kept alive
206 Higham, p 261

After the war, Colonel Eugene Bird[207] cooperated with Hess in writing a book seeking to set out the truth of Hess's mission. Bird's treatment by the US authorities gives the impression of a secret so monstrous that it could never be released[208]. The book makes no mention of the Final Solution or of Hess's remorse, as if the author had been warned off.

The possibility that Hess and Churchill could have saved the Jews is indeed dramatic and serious. Probably Hess was wise enough to know that Britain would not consider peace, or even negotiations unless he had something major to offer. And he knew Hitler well enough to know that he could not propose German withdrawal from Poland and Czechoslovakia. But there is another possibility, also disturbingly dramatic and serious, that had to be hushed up. Hess's draft peace treaty might even have proposed to **replace Hitler and Churchill**. Churchill always refused to negotiate with 'that man', and chose to present the war in very personal terms, seeming to blame everything on Hitler personally. Churchill might have negotiated with a different German leader, and there were certainly senior people in Germany who wanted to depose Hitler. Similarly, but perhaps more realistically, Hitler saw the war in personal terms, and blamed it on Churchill and his clique; he believed that there was a strong peace party in Britain. It is just possible that Hess was caught up in a plot to end the war by getting rid of both leaders. It was clear that he wanted to talk to King George VI and the Lord Steward of his Household[209], rather than Churchill and his clique, and he was not allowed to. He was under the impression that the King could dismiss Churchill and appoint another Prime Minister who was more in favour of a negotiated peace.

---

207 Secker and Warburg, 1974
208 Padfield, p 349
209 Air Commodore Douglas Hamilton, 14th Duke of Hamilton (1903-73), formerly known as Clydesdale, Lord Steward of King's Household 1940-64

Hess's well-known devotion and loyalty to Hitler make it unlikely that he would betray his Fuhrer. But his increasing disquiet at Nazi excesses, and knowledge of the proposed death camps, made his position more uncomfortable, and may have led him to seek dramatic action. It may even be that he was unwittingly caught up in a plot.

The presumption that Hess came at the invitation of Stewart Menzies with the agreement of Canaris for the purpose of toppling Hitler – although it is unlikely that Hess was unaware of that – is probably as close as possible as it is to approach the truth[210].

Picknett et al[211] examine possibilities more closely, and conclude:

... on the face of it, it seems outrageous to suggest that Hitler might have colluded in his own removal from office. But there is no doubt that Hess must have known that those with whom he discussed his peace proposals in Britain would have demanded the removal of Hitler. Perhaps Hess had come to formulate some kind of compromise – such as making Hitler the figurehead President of Germany, whilst he took over as Chancellor.

Whatever the truth may be in each of the above suggestions, it seems that Churchill and Roosevelt deliberately hushed up the proposals because they wanted to continue with the war.

Some authors have assembled a considerable body of evidence of networks of nobility and royalty, British, German and other, meeting and discussing the possibility of Peace. The Duke of Kent, for example, regularly went to see his wife's family in German controlled parts of Europe, well-connected to the Nazis. There is also clear evidence that Hitler wanted to be on good terms with the British royal family.

---

210 Padfield, p 361
211 Picknett et al, *Hess,* p 501

Picknett et al have also assembled a substantial body of evidence suggesting that the visit of Rudolf Hess (Hitler's deputy) to Britain on 10 May 1941 was pre-arranged with the expectation that he would meet King George VI, intending to sign a Peace Treaty with Britain. They suggest that a fair number of highly placed individuals had conspired to arrange this (including the Duke of Kent, the Duke of Hamilton, and many of their relatives). Churchill would probably not have agreed to this, and the plot may have involved the possibility of the King appointing a different Prime Minister. Arrangements must have been made, involving a fair number of people, perhaps including MI6, for Hess's plane to fly safely through British defences to Glasgow. In the event, it all went horribly wrong. Hess had to bail out near his intended destination and was arrested by the Home Guard and then imprisoned for the rest of his long life. Churchill found out (if he did not already know), and the full story has never been told. Full explanations and detailed files have still not been released (more than 70 years afterwards), and there have been suggestions that this could be to cover up the Royal Family's involvement. It seems that both the British and the Germans have been happy to collude with the idea that Hess was mad, and his venture did not involve anyone else.

But Churchill did not want a negotiated peace. He was determined to fight on, and wanted America to help him. It was a desperate gamble (which did not save Poland, or anyone else). By 1941 Britain was bankrupt and dependent on US assistance. If it now accepted a compromise peace with Hitler, it would lose all American help in the form of munitions, raw materials, and food. In these circumstances even home defence, and the maintenance of adequate levels of food for the population and raw materials for industry, would be difficult. It was as if there was no alternative but to carry on and hope for US intervention before it was too late.

Whatever the truth about Hess may be, it is clear that, in the early stages of the War, there was a significant faction in Britain in favour of negotiating peace, rather than continuing war with Germany.

A month after Hess's trip (10th June 1940), Italy declared war on Britain and France, and invaded South East France.

Churchill chose to continue with the war after May 1940 mainly to prevent Hitler from having 'overlordship' over Eastern Europe. 'Overlordship' is a strange and ill-defined concept. Churchill was in favour of British 'overlordship' in India, and much of Africa and South East Asia, perhaps even thinking that the 'Aryan' British race was superior to the black- and brown-skinned people over which they ruled. Hitler had comparable views about Slavs and Jews being inferior, and the superior German Aryan race having the right (or duty) to rule over them.

There was thus an element of hypocrisy in Churchill's (and so Britain's) stand. There was also an element of pig-headedness. Britain was simply not strong enough to impose its will over Europe. Stalin beat Hitler, and gained overlordship over Eastern Europe. Britain became dependent on America, who joined the war for her own advantage, and gained a form of overlordship over Britain and the British Empire.

5. Duke of Kent's Flying Accident

By the end of 1941, Churchill had achieved the support of the Cabinet for the pursuit of the war, and had been joined by Russia and the USA in a powerful and potentially winning alliance. Continuing with the war seemed inevitable, and significant attempts at a negotiated peace had more or less faded away.

There was, however, a mysterious incident that took place on August 25, 1942 which may indicate that there were powerful people in

Britain who still actively sought Peace. The official story was that a Sunderland flying boat, bound for a goodwill visit to Iceland, carrying 15 passengers including the Duke of Kent (King George VI's younger brother), took off from Invergordon on the east coast of Scotland. About 60 miles after take-off it crashed on the hill Eagles Rock, Caithness, in low cloud. Fifteen bodies were recovered.

There are many mysteries about this, and much speculation and suggestions of conspiracies of various kinds, but the following seem to be clear:

1. If the plane was really going to Iceland (and not somewhere like neutral Sweden, to the east) it should have taken off from the (safer) west coast of Scotland, not the east.
2. For some reason the route of the plane was altered at the last minute; it should have flown continuously over the sea, and not turned inland. The pilots were some of the best, and were unlikely to make such a mistake. The amended route seems to have been deliberate.
3. Although 15 people embarked on the plane, and 15 bodies were found, there was one survivor. He wandered off, dazed, for a day, and it seems was subsequently sworn to secrecy. There were therefore 15 dead passengers[212], plus one survivor. Nothing has been published officially to indicate who the extra body was.
4. The Duke of Kent had, handcuffed to him, a brief case containing a lot of Swedish currency, which would have been of no use in Iceland.
5. It seems that the plane was probably painted white, not the usual camouflage colours of the RAF.
6. The plane took about an hour longer than it should have done to

---

212 It is possible that the bodies were counted inaccurately in the mess and confusion; if there were supposed to be 15 bodies, the investigators may have thought they found 15 although there were only 14

cover the 60 miles, as if it had stopped off somewhere in north east Scotland.

Some of the less likely speculation suggests that the plane had landed on a lake on Archibald Sinclair's estate and picked up Rudolf Hess – who was subsequently replaced by a double, who lived until 1987[213]. The plane seems to have picked up someone, somewhere, and to have been on some sort of special mission, perhaps involving peace negotiations somewhere other than Iceland.

Many theories and speculations are beyond belief. Perhaps the 'accident' had been deliberately 'arranged' to dispose of a royal who did not want more war with Germany. The plane may well have crashed because it was unable to climb steeply enough over mountains and rocks, perhaps it had been interfered with, and it was intended to kill the unconventional Duke of Kent who was becoming a problem. But who knew that it would take the route that it did, instead of remaining over the sea? And why kill 14 other people – or were the rest of the crew knowingly killing themselves for the greater glory of Winston Churchill? It all seems very unlikely.

It was most likely an accident, perhaps on some sort of peace mission. Although in public Churchill always wanted to continue with the war, it should not be surprising that some individuals, with or without his knowledge, continued to explore possibilities of negotiations.

Why did Churchill Want to Continue with War?

It is worth speculating why Churchill wanted to continue with the war. It was consistent with his years of pre-war rhetoric which was

---

213 He met his son and wife a number of times while in Spandau; it is beyond belief that a double would want to spend the rest of his life in prison, or be able to delude the wife and son of Hess

pro-rearmament and anti-Hitler. It was essential for his political survival; much of the Conservative Party was anti-Churchill, and saw him only as a necessary evil to fight the war. If he gave up on the war, his political career would be finished; he would be 'torn from his place' if he tried to make peace with Germany in May /June 1940. Furthermore it should be remembered that much of his earlier life was imbued with anti-German feelings from WW1. He did not want to be a pale shadow of his friend and rival, Lloyd George, the great First World War Leader. Moreover, he had seen how reputation, fame and glory could come from success in war, both in his own life, and in that of his illustrious ancestor, Marlborough.

Britain had been at war with Germany, supposedly as a result of the Polish Guarantee, since September 3rd 1939. To start with it had only been a 'Phoney War', with little happening. Then, on April 9, 1940 Germany had begun to occupy Denmark and invade Norway (which capitulated a month after Churchill became Prime Minister). The British Expeditionary Force (BEF) had fought alongside the French, lost, and been isolated, and were making their way back to the Channel coast in the hope of evacuation. It was not possible to know how many, if any, of them would be rescued. The German forces could easily have defeated them, but Hitler held back. Perhaps he wanted to negotiate rather than to destroy British fighting forces. Hitler invaded Belgium, the Netherlands and Luxembourg on the very day that Churchill became Prime Minister. A few days later the Netherlands surrendered; the evacuation of Dunkirk began, and it was another four weeks before Churchill knew that the majority of the BEF had survived (without much of its equipment). On June 14 the Germans entered Paris, and the French signed an Armistice on June 22. Britain was alone, without significant allies in Europe, but she and Churchill survived long enough to claim to have won the war. It is that on which Churchill's reputation rests.

He was also in a weak position politically. Chamberlain was still

Leader of the Conservative Party. On the first day that Churchill, the new Prime Minister, appeared in the House of Commons, it was Chamberlain, not Churchill, who was cheered by Conservative MPs. Churchill was more popular with the Labour Party. But Churchill was dependent on the Conservative Party, and so on Chamberlain too.

It was clear that he wanted fame and glory.

'Total victory' thus became Government policy at Churchill's insistence, not because it was a practical possibility in the foreseeable future, but to shore up Churchill's support among Conservative backbenchers.

Chapter 8
The consequences
of World War 2

The consequences of WW2 include the following:

a. Deaths and Injuries
b. Destruction
c. Financial Costs
d. Effects on International Relations
e. Effects on Attitudes and Opinions

a. Deaths and Injuries

On May 22, 2013 Private Lee Rigby was hacked to death in a public street in Woolwich. It was a despicable and vicious murder which sent shockwaves throughout Britain. On March 8, 2014 Malaysia Airlines flight 370 disappeared with 239 people on board – all now presumed to be dead. The mystery of its disappearance filled newspaper headlines for weeks. Most people can visualise and identify with a plane-full of people and seem to understand and be shocked by a (relatively) small number of deaths. But when hundreds or thousands are killed, they seem to lose their shock value and become just statistics. In WW2 the number of deaths is beyond comprehension. It was not dozens, or hundreds, or thousands, or tens of thousands, or hundreds of thousands, or millions; it was tens of millions. In addition there were millions of people injured. A summary of deaths in Europe is included at the end of this Chapter.

Although this book is primarily concerned with Europe, it is worth recording that the largest numbers of deaths were in Russia (over 22 million), China (over 10 million), Germany (over 7 million) and

Poland (over 5 million). Millions were also killed in the Dutch East Indies, Japan and India.

In all perhaps as many as 60 million people were killed in WW2, around 3% of the world's population at the time.

These figures are horrific, and almost unbelievable. Many people in Britain are concerned about the many British lives that were lost. Indeed, 451,000 is an enormous number. But 10 countries lost far more, in some cases many times more.

Russia, Poland and Lithuania lost about 15% of their populations; Latvia, Germany, Greece and Yugoslavia lost around 10%. Around 1% of the population was lost in the UK, France and Italy. Denmark lost 'only' a tenth of one percent of their population.

The Holocaust was responsible for the deaths of about six million Jews – more than half of all Europe's Jews. The biggest numbers of Jews killed (included in the above totals), and their country of residence before the war were as follows:

Poland nearly 3 million (about 90% of the Jewish population)

Russia about 1 million (about one third of the Jewish population)

Hungary 5-600,000 (over 70% of the Jewish population).

Twenty five percent or more of the Jews (and in some cases 80% or more) were killed in Austria, Belgium, Czech Republic, Estonia, France, Germany, Greece, Hungary, Latvia, Lithuania, Luxembourg, Netherlands, Norway, Poland, Romania, Slovakia and Yugoslavia; and almost 25% in Russia.

The only German-controlled countries in which more than three quarters or more of the Jewish population survived were Germany (around 75%), Italy (about 83%), and Denmark (about 99%).

Appendix I at the end of this Chapter shows numbers of deaths, by (European) country. A number of themes emerge:

1. The countries with the largest populations had the most deaths with millions dying in Germany, Poland and the Soviet Union. Italy, France and the UK emerged with a smaller proportion of the population killed.
2. Neutral countries tended to lose the smallest proportions of their population, particularly Ireland, Spain, Sweden, Switzerland and Turkey.
3. Countries which put up little resistance also lost relatively small proportions of their populations, for example Albania, Austria, and Denmark.
4. The biggest proportionate losses (not surprisingly) were where there was most fighting, and/or where most Jews were killed, for example Estonia, Germany, Greece, Hungary, Latvia, Lithuania, Poland, the Soviet Union and Yugoslavia.

The lessons are fairly clear. If political leaders want to protect their populations, they are better not to fight, and preferably to remain neutral. Those who fight most (usually on some sort of 'principle'), lose most and thus betray their populations.

b. Destruction

WW2 brought massive destruction. Britain lost 260 major warships plus hundreds (perhaps thousands) of smaller naval vessels and merchant ships; 42,000 aircraft; 20,000 tanks; many thousands of transport vehicles, guns, ammunition, and smaller items of equipment; and fuel and supplies. In addition bombing destroyed transport infrastructure, manufacturing capacity (about 12% was lost) and, of course, homes. There was the Blitz in London, but also bombing in many other towns and cities throughout Britain. Coventry, Merseyside and Hull were particularly badly hit. The heart was ripped out of many cities and towns with large areas reduced to rubble. Even ten years after the war I remember that much of Bristol was still in ruins, and the rebuilding of the centre of the city had only just begun.

About two million houses were damaged beyond repair and over 60,000 British civilians were killed in the bombing, with perhaps twice as many injured.

It is easy to skip over these statistics and forget that each one was a tragedy for individuals and their families. Each one was a young child left without a home or parents, or a crippled mother, or an old man trapped with broken legs under a fireplace, or a pregnant mother, or a newly widowed mother who had just lost her last child, or a fatherless family with nowhere to go in the cold, rain and snow of winter, a professional person who lost everything, or a working person who had nothing, or a baby with no access to milk, or a child left to care for crippled parents, and so on. They were not just statistics.

Deaths and destruction in Germany were far worse because the Allies bombed Germany much more than Germany bombed Britain. One of the worst examples was Dresden: about 25,000 people were killed; 78,000 dwellings were completely destroyed, 27,700 made uninhabitable, and 64,500 damaged but repairable. It is easy to read these numbers coldly. More specific numbers sometimes give a more realistic picture: 640 shops, 31 large hotels, 19 hospitals and clinics, 39 schools and much more were destroyed. It is difficult to grasp a picture of a whole city becoming a fireball. More than 20,000 were killed in Berlin, and 40,000 at Hamburg, with, of course, equivalent injuries, damage and destruction.

In all about 500,000 civilians were killed by Allied bombing in Germany – nine times as many as in Britain, and 7,500,000 were made homeless. There were at least as many injuries as deaths. War led to wrecked lives, whether through physical or mental disablement, broken families or alcoholism. Bombs wrecked homes too. In Germany Allied bombing attacked about 61 towns and cities, and 20% of all homes were destroyed. Berlin was 70% destroyed by bombing; Dresden was 75% destroyed. Twenty or more German cities were "destroyed" by Allied bombing; one city (Coventry) in Britain is described as being "destroyed"[214].

It is significant that at least three major European cities (Paris, Prague, Copenhagen) were hardly affected by bombing. This is because those countries chose not to engage in major fighting, and so preserved their cities and people.

c. Financial Costs

It is difficult to say what the cost of WW2 was to Britain. Some estimate something of the order of $2,000,000,000,000 (in today's prices) – enough to finance the NHS for 5-10 years, or perhaps £100,000 per family.

It is difficult to establish exactly what such figures are supposed to include, and to be sure how adjustments have been made for inflation and changing exchange rates. A further problem is that some costs would have been incurred anyway, whether or not there was a war, and there was continuing renewal and replacement of ever-more sophisticated planes and other weaponry. Moreover there were non-financial costs and benefits which were more important: the human cost, Britain's place in the world, remarkable advances in technology, the replacement of tired old facilities with modern ones, and the

---

214 Wikipedia

near-destruction of Nazism. There is also the problem of double counting: the destruction of ships, aircraft and so on is a significant cost; but if they were financed by Lend-Lease from America, the cost of that should not be counted twice. There is also the question of what value should be put on supplies from America ($31.4 billion), given that Britain usually paid only a very modest part of the price, but also allowed America 99 year leases on bases that were part of the British Empire.

Although it is not possible to establish a precise, generally-agreed cost, it was clearly far more than Britain could afford; it bankrupted the country, and Britain was still paying off overseas debts until 50 years later. The National Debt (owed to British citizens) increased to more than 200% of GDP during the war; it went down to 25% by 1990 (but has increased to 50-70% since).

Government spending rose from less than 30% of GDP before the war to more than 60% during the war. The number of families paying income tax increased from 3.8 million before the war to 14.5 million afterwards. The percentage of government spending devoted to Defence was about 50% during the war (declining to about 25% afterwards).

It seemed that, during the war, the government financed as much of the costs as it could from general taxation. The war was financed from:

1. General taxation, but this was not enough, so also
2. Selling off assets (sometimes at knock down prices); and
3. Begging and Borrowing, mainly from the USA. According to Dimbleby and Reynolds, matters came to a head in October 1940 when the Treasury reported to Churchill that within three months the country would have no more money to buy equipment and supplies from America.

Britain's potentially weak financial position had been recognised within Whitehall before the war began. In July [1939] they pointed out that sustaining a three-year war (then Britain's military assumption) "is very likely much too optimistic". By February 1940, the Treasury thought that British resources might last between two and three years if they were carefully husbanded. That estimate turned out to be over-optimistic. The demands of the armed forces were higher than expected, the mass of equipment lost at Dunkirk had to be replaced, and when France had gone out of the war, their orders in the United States were taken over by Britain.

At the beginning of 1940 Britain had £775 million gold and dollar reserves, and saleable investments in the USA. Less than eight months later they had fallen to £490 million. It had been hoped that they would last until June 1941, but recent substantial orders meant that they would last no more than 3-4 months, and Britain would no longer be able to finance the war.

Britain's desperate straits were recognised by the Cabinet; they were determined to carry on with the war, knowing that Britain could not pay for it, and decided to wait and hope for American help. They even considered requisitioning all gold objects from people in Britain and recognised that it might be necessary to hand over the ownership of the whole of British industry to the Americans.

In many ways Britain was no longer operating as an independent nation; its fate would be decided by America.

It is not unusual for politicians to be posturing on the world stage, supposedly powerful because of weapons that the country cannot afford. In the 2015 general election, it was suggested that the Trident programme would cost £100 billion over 40 years – enough to finance all A&E departments in hospitals for 40 years.

In response to Britain's financial situation, Roosevelt pushed through the Lend-Lease Bill which enabled the USA to provide equipment and supplies to the Allies – on credit. But, first Britain had to hand over £50 million of gold from South Africa, and dispose of other overseas assets (eg Viscose [Courtaulds USA] was sold to a consortium of American bankers – who soon sold it again for a handsome profit).

America, with its strong non-interventionist policy (in early 1941) could not be seen to give financial aid and equipment to the UK. Supplies to the UK were made, often at a 90% discount, Britain having the option to return the equipment that had been loaned. But, at the end of the war, when the agreement came to an end, Britain retained much equipment, owing 10% of its 'value' to the USA, amounting to $1,075 million; this became a loan, with interest at 2%, and was finally repaid in 2006. Whilst some have seen this as generous, and it was certainly essential for Britain to continue with the war, it also had advantages for America.

- It boosted American manufacturing industry; indeed, there were significant pro war pressures from American armaments manufacturers;
- America gained the use of some British bases;
- The Americans gained from some British research and technological expertise;
- Without America's support Britain might not have survived as an independent nation, and might not have been able to repay anything.

A rough estimate might be that the out-of-pocket costs of the war to Britain were (in current prices) of the order of at least £20,000 per household, and perhaps as much as £100,000.

Taylor[215] states, regarding Britain's position at the end of the war:

Great Britain had drawn on the rest of the world to the extent of £4,198 million ... [and] Something like 10% of the pre-war national wealth had been destroyed, say £1,700 million, some by physical destruction, the rest by running down capital assets.

That would make a total cost of £5,898 million, excluding the costs of fighting the war that were born by the British taxpayer. That would amount to about £500 per household, which would have been enough to buy a decent house at the time.

Before the war, Britain was building about 300,000 houses a year. During the war virtually none were built – a loss of 1,800,000 houses. A typical 1930s semi-detached house is still a good, much sought after, decent house. Average house prices were typically around £500 before the war. After the war house-building was slow to recover. It eventually peaked at 300,000 per annum in the 1960s, then steadily declined to around half that rate.

Britain has a serious housing problem. Homeowners become richer as prices rise. Prices continue to rise as there are not enough houses. Young people are compelled to rent from private landlords. Many of those young people might dismiss WW2 as being the equivalent of ancient history; of no interest; nothing to do with them. But much of the current housing crisis can be blamed on WW2. About 1,800,000 homes were not built – even more if we consider the 20 years after the war, when there were still shortages, and house-building was restricted. Many homes were destroyed by bombing during the war. Moreover, the Government chose to spend an enormous sum on the war – enough to finance a home for every family in Britain.

---

215 A J P Taylor, *Oxford*, p 599

When young people today search for a flat at an affordable rent, that they may have to share with others, they should consider whether Britain should have spent more on house-building than on warmongering.

d. Effects on International Relations

Important effects of WW2 on international relations were:

- The world came to be dominated by two Great Powers: the USA and the Soviet Union. Britain and France were reduced to the rank of second rate powers, although they liked to think otherwise, and chose to maintain a world role and to develop nuclear weapons.

In the immortal words of Sellar and Yeatman:

America was thus clearly top nation, and History came to a. (full stop) [216]

- The British Empire and Commonwealth was undermined or destroyed. Britain, crippled by debt, simply could not afford to defend it all. Each nation of any size soon gained its independence from Britain and most of what was left of it was subject to the powerful influence of the USA. The Americans seemed able to establish military bases wherever they wished on 'British' soil: bases in Trinidad, Bermuda, and Newfoundland were given in return for 50 mothballed destroyers.[217] Diego Garcia, and Ascension Island were taken over subsequently; the British were not able to act independently of America (eg over Suez in 1956); and it seemed that the Americans could do almost

---

216 Sellar and Yeatmen, p 123; they were referring to WW1, but the comment could easily be applied to WW2
217 Johnson, p 251

whatever they wished on 'British' territory (eg 1983 American invasion of Grenada). Some argue that the loss of Empire was a by-product of a hopelessly expensive war; some see that the Americans deliberately undermined the Empire so that they could become the dominant world power; others see the end of the British Empire as inevitable, as different nations chose to rule themselves.

- Germany was divided between West Germany (pro NATO) and communist East Germany (which included the old, but officially divided, capital Berlin.) The two parts of Germany became re-united in 1990. It was soon recognised as the biggest and most populous country in Europe. If it had been accepted as such a century earlier, two world wars might have been avoided.

e. Effects on Attitudes and Opinions

Many leading Nazis were tried at Nuremberg for war crimes, particularly for participation in the Holocaust.

To the British people, who had sacrificed so much, it made it all seem worthwhile. The Nazis were cruel and wicked people who murdered millions of Jews and others, and they had to be stopped. The British people could feel good because they had done the right thing by fighting the Nazis in WW2.

They conveniently forgot why they had gone to war in the first place.

- Britain did not go to war to save the Jews.
- Britain did not save the Jews.
- Britain went to war to protect the independence of Poland.
- Britain did not protect the independence of Poland.

Millions of Jews had been killed. The Soviets controlled Poland. Indeed, the Soviets controlled most of Eastern Europe.

An important and terrible principle had been established: if one country thinks that another country is doing wrong, it can intervene in that country, declare all-out war, and do its best to destroy and humiliate that country. There is no need for international approval through the League of Nations or the United Nations.

Many people think that Communism is wrong. Many think that Capitalism is wrong. If one nation thinks it is acceptable to declare war on the other and aim for total destruction, we have a dreadful future ahead of us. Perhaps the warmongers will destroy us all.

In the years after WW2 Britain was bankrupt and no longer capable of undertaking such action. But the USA could and did. If Britain was right to declare war on Germany, over Poland, without League of Nations approval, then the USA is right to declare war on anyone it thinks is wrong (eg Communists or Muslims) without international approval. Since WW2 there have been a number of such terrible American-led wars.

The Table below illustrates how America has come to dominate the world with massive expenditure on armaments.

Although America and Russia are usually thought of as the two super-powers, America spends eight times as much as Russia on armaments. Although Britain and France might still wish to be seen amongst the 'big boys', they each spend only about one tenth of what America spends.

Twenty First Century Military Expenditure of Major Countries

Country	Annual Expenditure on Armaments $billion
USA	581
China	129
Saudi Arabia	81
Russia	70
UK	62
France	53
Japan	48
India	45
Germany	44
South Korea	34

Institute for Strategic Studies 2015

As we saw with Poland, the situation was much more complex than Right versus Wrong. There are no saints. It is always worth further negotiations to prevent war and its dreadful consequences. Between the First and Second World Wars many people were more idealistic, with widespread support for the League of Nations and Pacifism. The Second World War destroyed all that, and Pacifism became a dirty word. The warmongers had won.

The British might smugly think that they were right in WW2; or they may not be able to cope with thinking otherwise. But they established a terrible principle that might one day destroy the world.

Loss of Life in European Countries WORLD WAR 2

Country	Population 1/1/1939	Total Deaths	% Population	Jewish Pop. 1/1/1939	Jews killed	% Jews killed
Albania	1,073,000	30,000	2.7	-	-	-
Austria	6,653,000	124,000	1.8	191,000	50k-65,000	30.1
Belgium	8,387,000	88,000	1.0	60,000	77k-78,300	45
Bulgaria	6,458,000	21,500	0.33	-	-	-
Czech Rep.	10,400,000	325,000	3.15	92,000	77k-78,000	84.4
Denmark	3,795,000	6,000	0.16	8,000	60-116	1.1
Estonia	1,134,000	67,000	5.9	4,600	1.5k-2,000	38
Finland	3,700,000	85,000	2.3	-	-	-
France	41,680,000	600,000	1.44	260,000	75k-77,000	29.2
Germany	69,300,000	5,700,000	8.23	566,000	135k-142k	24.5
Greece	7,222,000	507k-807k	7-11.2	73,000	59k-67,000	86.3
Hungary	9,129,000	564,000	6.18	725,000	502k-569k	73.9
Iceland	118,900	200	0.17	-	-	-
Ireland	2,960,000	100	0.00	-	-	-
Italy	44,394,000	444,500	1.00	48,000	6.5k-9,000	16.1
Latvia	1,994,500	220,000	11.03	95,000	70k-72,000	74.7
Lithuania	2,575,000	345,000	13.4	155,000	130k-143k	88.1
Luxembourg	295,000	5,000	1.69	3,500	1k-2,000	42.9
Malta	269,000	1,500	0.06	-	-	-
Netherlands	8,729,000	210,000	2.41	112,000	100k-105k	91.5
Norway	2,945,000	10,200	0.35	1,700	800	47.1
Poland	34,849,000	5.9m-6m	16.9-17.2	3,250,000	2.7m-3m	87.7
Romania	15,970,000	500,000	3.13	441,000	121k-287k	46.3
Soviet Union	168,525,000	27,000,000	16.02	2,825,000	700k-1.1m	31.9
Spain	25,637,000	-	-	-	-	-
Sweden	6,341,000	2,100	0.03	-	-	-

Switzerland	4,210,000	100	0.00	-	-	-
Turkey	17,370,000	200	0.00	-	-	-
UK	47,760,000	450,900	0.94	-	-	-
Yugoslavia	15,490,000	1.03m-1.7m	6.63-10.97	68,000	56k-65k	89

Chapter 9
The morality of war

As most countries in Europe regarded themselves as being Christian, the first part of this chapter is concerned with the theory of a 'just war' as set out in the Roman Catholic Catechism. The views of other Christians are then considered. Towards the end of the Chapter the views of some other religions on war and violence are summarised[218].

Two commonly held views are sometimes used to justify WW2:

1. The right of self-defence,
2. What we are opposing is so evil, we must use all means, including war to stop it.

Each of these arguments will be dealt with separately.

1. The right of self defence

The case for individuals defending themselves against aggressors is different from countries defending themselves. Whatever individuals do is a matter for them, and the law. Others may or may not choose to become involved. Many people argue against pacifism, saying that if anyone attacks them they have the right to fight back. This book is not concerned with what individuals may choose to do.

The case for nations defending themselves against aggressors is very different because others, sometimes whole nations, have no choice but to become involved. They may be bombed, with deaths, injuries, and homes destroyed. They may be called on to do national service and to fight and kill. They may have to work in factories producing

---

218 Largely taken from the BBC website

armaments. They may find it difficult to obtain food or even be forced to starve to death. Their liberties are likely to be restricted, and many liberties may be suspended (including freedom of speech, and voting in general elections).

The decision of politicians to take a country to war is likely to be very far reaching. The decision of individuals to defend themselves when attacked is very different.

There are some similarities between individuals and nations. Sometimes individuals choose not to fight, because they know they cannot win. If I were to be attacked by an individual twice as strong as me, and half my age, I would not fight back; I could not win. I would either try to run away, appeal for help, or try to appease my attacker, and give what I had to, and my priority would be to survive. That would be appeasement, which is sometimes necessary.

If a small nation is attacked by another which is much bigger and stronger, there are few choices. They could not run away; they can try to appeal for help from other nations – but any help tends to be slow and unreliable, close to being hopeless. They could fight and lose – which some nations did in WW2. Or they could try appeasement, the idea which has since been unfairly discredited. A better option would be to try to live in peace, and co-operate and be friendly with their neighbours.

Throughout history there have been wars, often based on religious nationalism, and deriving from dynastic disputes, or disputes over territory and resources. The Church has often, reluctantly or otherwise, sanctioned such wars. Hundreds of years ago it mattered less because whole nations did not go to war; there was no need for innocent civilians to be involved. But everything changed with WW1 and the advent of mass bombing.

The Roman Catholic Church had set criteria for what could be accepted as a 'just war' for hundreds of years. Today these criteria are listed in Paragraph 2309 of their Catechism, a document which specifies their beliefs most clearly. The exact words of relevant paragraphs are reproduced below in **bold** followed by some discussion of each criterion.

The strict conditions for military defense by military force require rigorous consideration. The gravity of such a decision makes it subject to rigorous conditions of moral legitimacy. At one and the same time:

It is clear that there may be a case for defence, but any aggression or attack would not be moral.

It is also clear that all four of the criteria must apply for a war to be just.

1. **the damage inflicted by the aggressor on the nation or community of nations must be lasting, grave, and certain**

   In the case of WW2 the aggressor was assumed to be Germany, and the nation on which the damage was inflicted was Poland. When Britain declared war on Germany, the invasion was only two days old, and so the damage could not yet be called lasting, grave or certain.

2. **all other means of putting an end to it must have been shown to be impractical or ineffective**

   The British government would argue that this was the case, although attempts at negotiating a settlement continued until the last minute, and beyond.

3. there must be serious prospects of success

By May 1940, there was not a serious prospect of success. France had been invaded. The British Expeditionary Force was surrounded. There was no sign of more powerful allies.

In September 1939, Britain and France may have thought that there was a serious prospect of success as the combination of the two of them looked very powerful. Declaring war could be justified under this criterion. Eight months later continuing with the war could not be justified.

It could be argued that there must have been a serious prospect of success, because, ultimately, Germany was defeated. However, success came mainly as a result of two pieces of luck:

i.   Japan bombed Pearl Harbor, and so America came into the war; and

ii. Germany over-reached itself, invading Russia, and ultimately it was the Russians who drove the Germans out of Poland.

On 3rd Sept 1939, it would have been difficult to foresee these two pieces of luck, and it was easy to see that the distant nations of France and Britain would have needed to intervene promptly and in an overwhelming way, more so than they were willing to do, to have a serious prospect of success. At the beginning of the war, although Britain and France may have thought otherwise, there was no serious prospect of success. It did not therefore qualify as a 'just war' in accordance with the Church's third criterion.

4. **the use of arms must not produce evils and disorders graver than the evil to be eliminated. The power of modern means of destruction weighs very heavily in evaluating this condition**

This criterion applies more to the way in which a war is to be fought, rather than the case for fighting. Britain was prepared to fight with heavy bombers, pulverising German cities. This, and the ways in which the war was fought, were not in accordance with the criteria for a just war, and the war could not therefore be justified.

These are the traditional elements in what is called the "just war" doctrine

Although a case could be argued under each of the four criteria, it is far from clear that all four applied. It is difficult to argue that WW2 was a just war – if only because of the way in which it was conducted.

The catechism of the Roman Catholic Church makes a number of other statements which make it clear that killing in war is morally unacceptable, particularly killing of civilians. Extracts from the catechism are shown in **bold** below.

2262 In the Sermon on the Mount the Lord recalls the commandment 'You shall not kill', and adds to it the proscription of anger, hatred and vengeance. Going further, Christ asks his disciples to turn the other cheek, to love their enemies. He did not defend himself and told Peter to leave his sword in its sheath.

One evil act does not justify another. Violence begets violence. Meeting violence with violence does more harm than good.

Of course the Nazis killed many Jews and others. Stalin, Britain's ally, was responsible for even more deaths. The British killed many Germans and others. It may be that one side was worse than the others. But all of the main participants in the war were morally wrong, and their actions were not compatible with Christianity.

2263 The legitimate defence of persons and societies is not an exception to the prohibition against the murder of the innocent that constitutes intentional killing.

It is difficult to believe that there could be a war without intentional killing of the innocent (mainly by bombing).

2268 The fifth commandment forbids direct and intentional killing as gravely sinful

2303 ... Hatred of the neighbor is a grave sin when one deliberately desires him grave harm. "But I say unto you love your enemies and pray for those who persecute you, so that you may be sons of your Father who is in heaven."

2304 Respect for and development of human life require peace

2307... Because of the evils and injustices that accompany all war, the Church insistently urges everyone to prayer and to action so that the divine Goodness may free us from the ancient bondage of war.

2308 All citizens and all governments are obliged to work for the avoidance of war.

2314 Every act of war directed to the indiscriminate destruction of whole cities or vast areas with their inhabitants

is a crime against God and man, which merits firm and unequivocal condemnation. A danger of modern warfare is that it provides the opportunity to those who possess modern scientific weapons, especially atomic, biological or chemical weapons, to commit such crimes.

Nations sometimes go into wars with the belief and intention that they will act morally, avoiding indiscriminate killing of civilians. But escalation happens too easily.

2315 The accumulation of arms strikes many as a paradoxically suitable way of deterring potential adversaries from war. They see it as the most effective way of ensuring peace among nations. This method of deterrence gives rise to strong moral reservations. The arms race does not ensure peace. Far from eliminating the causes of war, it risks aggravating them. Spending enormous sums to produce ever new types of weapons impedes efforts to aid needy populations; it thwarts the development of peoples. Over-armament multiplies reasons for conflict and increases the danger of escalation.

The table towards the end of Chapter 2 indicates the extent of re-armament in the years before WW2. It seems that re-armament did more to provoke war (through competitive re-armament) than it did to protect peace.

2316 The production and the sale of arms affect the common good of nations and of the international community. Hence public authorities have the right and duty to regulate them. The short term pursuit of private or collective interests cannot legitimate undertakings that promote violence and conflict among nations and compromise the international juridical order.

2327 Because of the evils and injustice that all war brings with it, we must do everything reasonably possible to avoid it. The Church prays "From famine, pestilence and war O Lord deliver us"

2329 "The arms race is one of the greatest curses on the human race and the harm it inflicts on the poor is more than can be endured"

2330 "Blessed are the peacemakers for they shall be called the sons of God"

The overwhelming flavour of the Roman Catholic Catechism is anti-war, anti-killing, anti- the arms race and pro-peace. War is seen as justified and necessary in some circumstances, but the criteria for a just war are hard to meet.

The Roman Catholic Church does not speak for all Christians, but other Christian churches are remarkably similar, deriving from the same roots, and based on the New Testament of the bible.

It is not difficult to find justification for revenge and war in the Old Testament (eg 'an eye for an eye and a tooth for a tooth' Exodus 21,24). But followers of Christ see that the New Testament is rather different.

You have heard that it was said 'eye for eye and tooth for tooth'. But I tell you Do not resist an evil person. If someone strikes you on the right cheek, turn to him the other also. And if someone wants to sue you and take your tunic, let him have your cloak as well... You have heard that it was said 'love your neighbour, hate your enemy'. But I tell you Love your enemies, pray for those that persecute you (Matthew 5, 38-44).

Jesus did not say that you should try to 'win' at all costs, and bomb millions of innocent people.

When they came to arrest Jesus,

*With that one of Jesus' companions reached for his sword, drew it out and struck the servant of the high priest, cutting off his ear. 'Put your sword back in its place,' Jesus said to him, 'for **all who draw the sword will die by the sword'**.* (Matthew 25, 51-2, emphasis added)

That could well be the pacifists' motto. Or, similarly, violence begets violence, the idea which was behind the abolition of capital punishment and of corporal punishment, and attempts to stop violence against children, and women. Violence is never the solution to a problem; it merely leads to more violence.

It seems clear that Jesus Christ would not have advocated the course of war undertaken by Britain, Churchill and America.

But, to retain acceptability, and to go along with the prevailing mood, the Church of England needed to sanction war. In the Church of England the just war theory had existed for many years. A war must have a just cause, be waged by a proper authority and with a right intention, be undertaken only if there is a reasonable chance of success and if the total good outweighs the total evil expected (overall proportionality). It must also be waged as a last resort and in pursuit of peace. Criteria are also set out for the conduct of war. These are discrimination (avoiding intentional harm to non-combatants) and proportionality of means (using such force as is essential to pursue the just cause).

The provenance of the just war theory and teaching of the Church of England (Anglican /Episcopalian) teaching on just war theory is the same as that of the Catholic Church. It is derived from the teachings of Jesus, and of Ambrose and Augustine in the fourth and fifth centuries, with the first coherent theory being developed by Gratian in the twelfth century. According to the Episcopal Church[219], the criteria for going to war – a just war – include the following:

Just cause; Just authority; right intention; last resort; public declaration; probability of success; and proportionality.

Most of these have already been discussed and have applied over the centuries. But the church has specified more clearly what is meant by proportionality – and in the context of modern warfare. Justice in the waging of war means two things:

- Proportionality with regard to the means of warfare rather than the ends; and
- Discrimination, or non-combatant immunity with regard to the damage to be caused by warfare.

Proportionality also means that the good to be achieved is greater than the evil to be suffered and inflicted.

Modern warfare, and the use of widespread bombing, cannot meet these criteria. The warmongers always try to argue that their bombing is 'precision' using 'surgical strikes'. But 'collateral damage' is inevitable, and there is no non-combatant immunity.

Some of the criteria for what constitutes a 'just war' are not exactly precise, and are difficult to interpret, even for those who are well-versed in these matters. Unfortunately it is the man on the Clapham Omnibus who has to fight, risk death and injury, and his family might be bombed or starved, or killed. But he is not in a good position to assess whether or not a forthcoming war meets the criteria of being

---

219 The Anglican Church in the USA – the head being the Archbishop of Canterbury

just. He may believe what his government tells him, but it is difficult to distinguish between truth and propaganda. The ordinary citizen cannot assess the chances of their side winning in a conflict: their political leaders tend to assure them that they are right, and can win, and defeat 'the baddies'; but then they would, wouldn't they? Political leaders make careers out of such ventures, and have little to lose.

The church does not oppose all wars in all circumstances, particularly those that are in self-defence. Poland may have been justified in fighting the German invasion of Poland[220]; and Britain may have been justified in helping Poland. But there are two problems with this argument:

i.   Britain did not help Poland. Britain wanted a war with Germany.
ii. Britain wanted to win at all costs, regardless of Poland, and engaged in saturation bombing of German cities. This was not allowable by the criteria for a just war.

Some might argue that Britain fought WW2 in defence of Britain. This ignores the fact that Germany did not attack, or even threaten to attack Britain, until after Britain had declared war on Germany.

2. What we are opposing is so evil, we must use all means, including war to stop it

This argument is quite distinct from the 'self- defence' argument, and rather different from the 'just war' argument, and is largely based on the Nazis' treatment of the Jews.

---

220 Although there was not a serious prospect of success; the German forces were so much more powerful, modern and effective. Horses cannot fight tanks. But the Polish government thought there was a serious prospect of success because of the guarantees from Britain and France

The four criteria for a 'just war' do not seem to be applicable here. The first applies only to a nation or community of nations, which the Jews were not. All other means of rescuing the Jews had not been shown to be impractical or ineffective. There was not a serious prospect of success. Moreover, the use of modern means of bombing leading to deaths and destruction seemed inevitable.

However, there is no doubt that the Holocaust was particularly evil, and that the Nazis, even in their early days, were violent, murderous, dictatorial and cruel. But the Holocaust did not justify going to war in 1939, because it had not happened, and had not even been planned at that time. As the war progressed, the Nazi regime became even more extreme, cruel and murderous.

Nevertheless, there was enough evidence about the cruelty of the Nazi regime before 1939 to provoke opposition to Germany in Britain. Kristallnacht (November 9-10, 1938) resulted in the deaths of hundreds of Jews, the burning of more than a thousand synagogues, the destruction of thousands of Jewish businesses, and the imprisonment in concentration camps of tens of thousands of Jews. The German government was an undemocratic, military dictatorship, suppressing civil liberties and positively anti-Semitic. It seems clear that Churchill, but by no means all British people, wanted to get rid of the Nazis. He wanted to achieve regime change.

There was a clear moral case for getting rid of the Nazis, but there are a number of problems with this:

1. While there is no doubt about the cruelty and disregard for life of the Nazi regime, even before 1939, there is no reason to suppose that it was the worst offender in eastern Europe.

    There were more dictatorships than democracies in central and eastern Europe; anti-Semitism was widespread; the German regime was probably no worse than the Polish regime; indeed, prior to 1938, Jews did relatively well in Germany. Stalin had already proved himself to be responsible for more deaths than Hitler.

Britain picked on Germany (supposedly because of Poland) and declared war. It might equally have picked on Poland or Russia (though Britain had no chance against Russia).

There was a moral case against Germany. Equally, there was a moral case against Britain's allies, Russia and Poland.

2. It may have been illegal. Churchill wanted to defeat and get rid of the Nazis. He wanted regime change, and to use force to implement it. It is now agreed that the use of force to achieve regime change in a country is generally illegal, even if the country is harming its own citizens, except with the approval of the United Nations. The position was less clear in the 1930s, before the United Nations existed. But even in the 1930s there was international law, including recognition of the nation state, which assumed that one nation was not allowed to interfere in the internal affairs of another nation. International institutions existed: there was the Permanent Court of Arbitration[221] (established in 1899 by the Hague Peace Conference to settle international disputes); there was the League of Nations established at the end of WW1 to maintain world peace through collective security and disarmament, and settling international disputes through negotiation and arbitration.

Hitler did not care for these international institutions; he simply

---

221 More than 100 countries were party to this, including the USA, Britain, France, Germany, the Russian Federation – and even Poland (after 1922; it was not recognised as a country until 1919)

marched into areas that had previously been German. Germany had a possible claim to these territories, but chose to use military superiority, as if 'Might is Right'.

The Allies seemed to assume that 'Mightier is Righter'.

Warmongers and politicians wanted to win and preserve their own positions and power.

Statesmen would have cared more about what would make the world a better place. Today it seems obvious that peace, negotiation, arbitration, co-operation, and the use of international institutions to settle disputes are better than war. But even after more than seventy years, there are still rogue nations (or politicians) that prefer wars – even if they are illegal.

3.   Although declaring war may have been intended to improve the position of Hitler's victims, it may have done just the opposite. It is not clear what Chamberlain and his colleagues thought the result of Britain and France declaring war might be. They might have hoped that Hitler would be so afraid of their pathetic[222] armies that he would refrain from invading Poland, withdraw from the former German territories that he had reclaimed, restore Parliamentary democracy in Germany and all of the thirty political parties which he despised, start being nice to the Jews, restore their businesses to them, un-burn down their synagogues and release all prisoners from the concentration camps. He did not, and they must have been potty if they thought he would do any of that.

---

222   The British army was too small to be effective against Germany. The French army showed no sign of being any more effective in defending France than it was in (not) defending Poland

Once war was declared, the position in Germany became worse in many ways. Emigration, which had been the Nazis' preferred option, became almost impossible for Jews; the war condemned them to annihilation. Many Germans patriotically rallied around the flag in defence of their homeland, against their British enemies. Allied bombing of Germany further entrenched this. In some ways the war might have strengthened Hitler's position in Germany[223]. It may also have led him to more extreme measures, including secret police, the SS, and the Holocaust.

4. It was none of Britain's business. Britain was not the policeman of the world. Other regimes were as bad elsewhere. It was not Britain's job to pick the worst, defeat them, and then to go on to the next worst. Any such role belonged to an international organisation such as the League of Nations. It was Britain's moral duty to strengthen international organisations, not to undermine them.

That may sound cruel and callous about the Jews. But the fact is that declaring war did no good to the six million Jews[224] who perished.

In the end, the war did some good for the few that survived. The pitiful survivors of the concentration camps, liberated at the end of the war, enabled most British people to believe that they had been right all along, right to fight the war and to defeat Nazism. They conveniently forgot the deaths and destruction of the war, the fact that it made Britain bankrupt, and the millions who had died while Britain concentrated on 'winning' the war rather than helping the victims of the Nazis.

---

223 Just as it strengthened Churchill's position in Britain
224 And millions of others

5. The war established the dreadful precedent that it is acceptable for a major country to declare war on and bomb a less powerful country, with no need for international approval. A number of wars have disastrously followed that precedent in subsequent years.

6. One of the arguments often used against Hitler is that he should not be allowed to obtain what he wanted by force[225]. Although that argument was used against Hitler, with reference to his invasion of Poland, it was never used against Stalin regarding his taking over of a large part of Poland. It is easy to say that there is a strong moral case for a particular international action; it seems impossible to stick to that principle in practice. The evidence of WW2 suggests that as the war progressed, each side became more extreme in murder, and in the bombing of civilians, in their determination to win at all costs; morality was ignored.

7. Regime change does not necessarily mean changing the government. It could be argued that Hitler personally was particularly bad; he should have been assassinated, and replaced by someone else. The problem was that his replacement might have been just as bad, or even worse. In the early years Hitler and the Nazis were reasonably popular and successful, as the Weimar Republic and democracy had not been; the Nazis' anti-Semitic lies and propaganda were effective: socialists and communists were condemned and even feared. Deposing Hitler would not have changed all that.

Regime change could also have meant making the regime more humane. Declaring war did not do that; it forced Hitler into a corner where his defensive behaviour became more extreme. Whilst some Germans had been brainwashed by the propaganda, and co-operated in the ill-treatment and murder of millions, most

---

225 As stated in Chamberlain's declaration of war

were either reluctant accomplices or ignorant of what was going on. Churchill knew what was going on as German codes had been broken; he did not declare what he knew because he wanted to keep it secret that he had access to German encoded information and wanted to use it to win the war. If Britain's priority had been to try to make Germany (and the world) more humane, and to rescue those who were suffering under the Nazis, there were better ways than all-out war, to be won at all costs. The worst abuses in the world cannot be stamped out by keeping them secret. A more moral approach than war would have been to disclose the abuses, in Germany and internationally, to campaign to have them stopped; to engage in international discussions, negotiations, arbitration and inspections, to publicise what was going on, and to campaign against anti-Semitism. Anti-Semitism was not defeated by defeating Hitler in war. Its proponents must have their arguments confronted head on.

Since 1945 there has been plenty of publicity and propaganda to show the world how appalling the Nazis were and, by implication, how wonderful Churchill and the Allies were. If the same effort had been put into publicising their abuses in the 1940s, much of it might have been avoided.

Clearly there was a very strong case against the Nazis, but that does not mean that an all-out war against Germany was the most appropriate response, or that it was justified.

There is no way in which the evils of war can be balanced against the evils that it might be intended to stop. Neither is known with any certainty, and actual results are always likely to turn out differently from what was intended. Similarly there is no way of showing that the Nazis should have been destroyed 'at all costs'. No-one knew what the costs would be. A more important question is: should anyone have the right to judge that a whole nation should be destroyed, and to risk everything in order to destroy that nation? Churchill seemed to assume that he had that right and managed to persuade[226] Parliament to support him.

We live in a world where many regimes and nations fall short of our ideals. But we do not go around saying that they should be destroyed at all costs because we – or someone – condemn them as evil. Many countries in the world are not Christian, not Democratic, or are homophobic, racist or sexist; many use cruel and unusual punishments, are too authoritarian or militaristic, or aggressive; or they are Communist or Muslim. But that is no reason to declare war on them or bomb them.

Most religions seem to be based on the idea of love being better than hate or war, and condemn killing or murder.

Sometimes religions seem to twist themselves inside-out to defend their participation in or support of particular wars.

Although most leading politicians in Britain paid lip-service to Christianity, many were not serious. Churchill did not even claim to be a Christian, although he did claim to be defending Christian values.

---

226   Or bully; a Prime Minister can usually rely on the bulk of his party's MPs supporting him. Most are usually in office, and would be sacked for not following the party line, or are very keen to be loyal so that they might soon be in office; the Whips are good at using their knowledge of Members' peccadillos to persuade them to support the Government for fear of disclosure. The argument was also used that Parliament needed to appear united so as not to give the Enemy the impression that they were weakening. There was also the threat from Regulation 18B

Other Religions

I. Islam

Although Muslims favour Jihad, or holy war, this is often misinterpreted. The Koran says:

Fight in the way of Allah against those who fight against you, but begin not hostilities.

Unfortunately there is often a dispute about who began hostilities. It is usually 'the other side' who started it. In WW2 it is usually accepted that Hitler began the hostilities, so presumably it was acceptable to fight against those hostilities.

The Koran also says:

But if the enemy incline towards peace, do thou also incline towards peace, and trust in Allah, for He is One that hears and knows all things.

At the beginning of WW2, Hitler made various peace offerings, and attempts to achieve peace. But the Allies did not trust him.

Hadith (Muslim oral tradition) also says:

Hate your enemy mildly; he may become your friend one day.

This seems to argue for any war being limited to defined objectives (eg to stop aggression and restore Polish independence), rather than totally destroying an enemy.

It is also said that a military Jihad has to follow strict rules in order to be legitimate:

1. The opponent must have started the fighting
2. It must not be fought to gain territory
3. It must be launched by a religious leader
4. It must be fought to bring about good, something Allah would approve of
5. It must be a last resort – all other ways of solving the problem must have been tried
6. Innocent people should not be killed – women and children or old people should not be killed or hurt
7. Women must not be raped or abused in any way
8. Enemies must be treated with justice
9. Wounded enemy soldiers must be treated in exactly the same way as one's own soldiers
10. The war must stop as soon as the enemy asks for peace
11. Property must not be damaged
12. Poisoning of wells is forbidden (chemical or biological warfare [or bombing] might be a modern analogy)

WW2 clearly breached many of these, particularly:

* It was not a last resort. In the first few months of the 'phoney war' it seems that neither Hitler nor Chamberlain wanted a war, but they did not manage to negotiate.

* Millions of innocent people were killed, particularly as a result of bombing.

Moreover, WW2 was not about defending Islam from attack, and there is no Muslim defence for it.

II. Hinduism

Hindus believe that it is right to use force in self-defence.

The Rig Veda (6-75:15) sets down the rules for war and says that a warrior will go to hell if he breaks any of them:

- Do not poison the tip of your arrow
- Do not attack the sick or old
- Do not attack a child or a woman
- Do not attack from behind

These rules were written before the age of mass bombing, which they would not have allowed. It is not possible to bomb a city without attacking the sick, the old, children and women.

Within Hinduism teachings about war and violence do vary. Some recognise that warriors have a duty to fight, and that violence affects only the body, not the soul; life and death are only an illusion, and it is the spiritual that matters. Others argue in favour of Ahisma, one of the ideals of Hinduism; this means: avoiding even the desire to harm any living thing, although even Gandhi did not equate Ahisma with non-killing; killing might be one's duty, but should be done in a detached way, without anger or selfish motives.

III. Buddhism

Non-violence is at the heart of Buddhist thinking and behaviour. The first of the five precepts that Buddhists should follow is:

Avoid killing or harming any living thing.

Nothing in Buddhist scripture gives any support to the use of violence in resolving disputes.

One of Buddha's sermons emphasises the requirement to love your enemy, no matter what:

Even if thieves carve you limb from limb with a double-handed saw, if you make your mind hostile, you are not following my teaching.

Buddhists (eg the Dalai Lama) say that hatred will not cease by hatred, but by love alone. Many Buddhists have refused to take up arms in any circumstances, even if they would be killed as a result. Rules for Buddhist monks allow them to defend themselves, but not to kill, even in self-defence.

Martial arts may appear violent, but there are strong spiritual and philosophical elements, and the emphasis is on the use of minimum violence to parry attacks.

Not all Buddhists have always lived up to such high idealism, and have at times engaged in wars (most recently in Sri Lanka).

IV. Judaism

Judaism does not accept that violence and war to protect justice is always wrong. But before starting war there must be a genuine attempt to make peace and to avoid the conflict. Jewish law permits only combatants to be deliberately killed in war; innocent civilians should be given every opportunity to leave the field of combat before a battle starts.

As with most other religions, before a war, there must be genuine peace-making attempts; mass killing of innocent civilians is not permitted.

V. Sikhism

Sikhism recognises five thieves, or five major human weaknesses: (i) lust (ii) rage (iii) greed (iv) attachment and (v) ego

The practising Sikh should subdue these; their minds should be above and beyond these inner urges.

But warmongers seem to be motivated by many of these.

Sikhs also recognise five virtues: (i) truth (ii) contentment (iii) compassion (iv) humility and (v) love.

One of the warmonger's first casualties is truth; he tends to show little compassion or love for his enemy, and generally lacks humility.

A good Sikh would be very much against the attitudes and motivations that are generally present in War Leaders and would heed the teaching:

Do good to him that hath done thee evil, and do not nurse anger in thy heart

But, as with most religious groups, Sikhs have participated in various wars over the centuries.

Conclusion

The moral codes of the major religions of the world with regard to war have much in common with each other. Overwhelmingly they preach love and conciliation rather than confrontation, war and killing. Also they generally condemn the killing of women, children and the elderly, and justify war only in self-defence. There is no religious defence for the mass bombing of cities, or for the murder of millions of Jews and others.

Religious leaders can legitimately argue in favour of war to defend their religions from attack. But neither Hitler not Churchill claimed that either of them was attacking or defending a particular religion. There are no religious or other moral codes that provide a case for

Britain fighting WW2 and bombing and killing women, the elderly, and children. Churchill's desire to win 'at all costs' destroyed any moral case that there may have been.

There are disagreements and different views within each religion; adherents of each have at times fallen short of their ideals, and engaged in wars. But most would probably agree that hate (and war) leads to more hate (and war); and that love is preferable.

It would be too simplistic to argue either that the Holocaust was a principal cause of WW2, or that WW2 was a cause of the Holocaust. But timing alone shows that the former could not be true.

Atomic bombs were dropped in Hiroshima and Nagasaki in August 1945

The war ended with 'Victory in Europe' (V-E) day, May 8th 1945, which was shortly after the Russians invaded Berlin and Hitler killed himself. 'Victory in Japan' (V-J) day, August 15th, followed shortly after the Americans used atomic bombs on Hiroshima and Nagasaki (without warning), killing over 100,000 people instantly, and many more over the following days, months and years.

Those who think that it was right for Britain to go to war in 1939 have two main arguments

1. We had to save Poland which had been invaded; and
2. We had to save six million Jews and others.

Both arguments fail because we did not save Poland, and we did not save six million Jews.

However, by using something like 'double-think', the warmongers manage to use two wrong arguments to support each other. The following conversation, between a pacifist and a warmonger, illustrate how these arguments can still be persuasive.

Warmonger: *We had to go war to save Poland*

Pacifist: *But we did not save Poland*

Warmonger: *No, but the Nazis were wicked and cruel, and we had to save the Jews*

Pacifist: *But we did not save the Jews. If we had not gone to war we could have helped them*

Warmonger: *But we had to go to war to save Poland*

Pacifist: *But we did not save Poland*

(That circular argument has continued for seventy years; an alternative version is shown below)

Warmonger: *The Nazis were wicked and cruel, and we had to save the Jews*

Pacifist: *Should we have tried to save the Jews in Poland and Russia too?*

Warmonger: *Poland and Russia were our allies in defeating the Nazis. Moreover, the Nazis invaded Poland*

Pacifist: *But the Russians invaded Poland too, sixteen days after Hitler did*

Warmonger: *We needed Russian help to defeat Germany, and to save the Jews (and to save Poland from Germany)*

Pacifist: *But we did not save the Jews, or Poland. We didn't even try ...*

Chapter 10
Myths and Generalisations

This chapter

I. Examines some myths that have grown up about WW2; and
II. Suggests some generalisations that apply to WW2, and to many other wars.

I. Myths

1. It was to help Poland – but little or no help was given. Britain declared war on Germany because Germany had invaded Poland, and Britain had 'guaranteed' Poland's independence. But a 'phoney' war followed, and Britain did nothing to help Poland. Moreover, Britain (but not Poland) was willing to accept most of Hitler's demands (regarding Danzig and the Polish Corridor) and the war could have been avoided.

2. It was to help the Jews. Many people and countries in Europe discriminated against, and were even cruel, to Jews; that was well known in Britain. But helping Jews in other countries was certainly not a priority for Britain. News of the slaughter of the Holocaust gradually seeped out in the later years of the war, but was nothing to do with Britain going to war. Britain could have helped the Jews, but instead chose the glory of total victory in the war, while six million Jews were slaughtered.

3. It was a personal struggle with Hitler. Each time when Churchill might justifiably have used the words 'Nazis' or 'Reich' or 'Germans', he concentrated on the person of Hitler. In response to his volte face in supporting Russia, Churchill said that he had only one purpose, the destruction of Hitler, who Churchill said

was 'a monster of wickedness, insatiable in his lust for blood and plunder'. But if the war had really been such a personal struggle, it would have been more effective to assassinate that one man, rather than millions being slaughtered. Of course it would have been difficult to assassinate him – many Germans tried (and sometimes almost succeeded), but he was lucky and he was well protected. The British made no serious attempt; they feared he might be replaced by someone worse. Clearly the enemy was not mainly the person of Hitler.

The tendency to personalise the conflict was reciprocated. Hitler said about the 'English':

Let us not forget, after all, that they owe all that's happening to them to one man, Churchill.

4. It was because Hitler was breaching the Treaty of Versailles. That was certainly influential in causing WW2. But others were breaking it too, and no-one followed its provisions requiring disarmament. Germany was clearly overthrowing the Treaty of Versailles by seizing mostly former German territory, but Poland also seized additional territory, yet they became Britain's ally, not Britain's enemy like Germany.

5. Hitler was threatening to invade Britain, and the war was necessary to prevent this. But the timing shows this to be a myth. Hitler did not plan or threaten to invade Britain until after Britain had declared war on Germany. It was Britain's declaration of war that provoked the plans. Churchill was not slow to use the possibility of a German invasion to mobilise British opinion in favour of the war. He said:

We are told that Herr Hitler has a plan for invading the British Isles ...
Even though large tracts of Europe and many old and famous states

have fallen or may fall into the grip of the Gestapo and all the odious apparatus of Nazi rule, we shall not flag or fail. We shall go on to the end, we shall fight in France, we shall fight on the seas and oceans, we shall fight with growing confidence and growing strength in the air, we shall defend our Island, **whatever the cost may be***, we shall fight on the beaches, we shall fight on the landing grounds, we shall fight in the fields and in the streets, we shall fight in the hills,* **we shall never surrender**[227] *[emphasis added].*

That was brilliantly stirring oratory, largely based on supposed invasion plans, which Britain had provoked, and which Churchill himself may not have believed. But it served to stir British people into action. It was also Churchill fighting for his own political position – against a negotiated peace.

6. The Germans bombed Britain and so Britain had to retaliate. The Germans were the first to bomb cities (in Warsaw, Norway and Holland), but these were limited campaigns in support of ground forces. British bombers were designed to bomb cities, whereas the Germans rejected this strategy and, at first, used bombing only to blast open a path for attacking armies. The decision to bomb civilians, repeatedly and on a massive scale, independently of any ground-based military operations, was taken by Churchill soon after he became Prime Minister. Hitler opposed this tactic and refused to retaliate for more than three months. He said on September 4, 1940 that he hoped Churchill would stop this nonsense.

British bombing of German cities began on 11 May 1940 (the day after Churchill was appointed Prime Minister) at Monchengladbach; Germany's bombing of Britain (The Blitz) began in September 1940.

---

227   House of Commons, 4 June 1940

Dresden after the bombing raid during WW2

Dresden was heavily bombed by Britain and America on 13-15 Feb 1945, shortly before the war ended, creating a firestorm over 1600 acres, destroying the city centre, and killing about 24,000 people.

7. The war was to save Civilisation, Democracy and Freedom for the world. Many such exaggerated claims have been made, as if Hitler was about to invade America, South Africa and Australasia.

Freedom in Britain had been severely restricted by Defence Regulation 38: British citizens were not even allowed to express opinions about whether the war could be won, and many foreign residents were interned. Churchill's views on democracy, and his own position, as an unelected political leader, were somewhat dubious. And it is a strange interpretation of the word 'Civilisation' if it is to include avoiding civilised negotiation, friendship and agreement, but instead, engaging in warmongering and saturation bombing of innocent civilians.

8. Britain's position was moral. In his declaration of war on September 3rd 1939 Chamberlain claimed the moral high ground – it was Right against Evil. But two Wrongs do not make a Right and even if Britain was perfect, she chose some very dubious allies. The suggestion that WW2 was simply the Good Allies against the Bad Axis Powers is far from the truth. Both were bad in their own ways, and going to war made the position worse.

9. The British government never considered anything other than total victory / defeat. It seemed reasonable to suggest that wars should end with a negotiated peace, rather than continuing with death and destruction until total defeat of the enemy. But that is what Churchill claims to have insisted on, although there were serious politicians who wanted a negotiated peace. Churchill bulldozed his way through such ideas and even tried to pretend that they never existed.

10. There was a cosy Alliance with our American friends that rescued Britain. It was not particularly friendly; America took what it wanted and was reluctant to enter the war. America acted in its own interests, did well out of manufacturing armaments for Britain and others, was happy to have military bases on British territory around the world. They 'saved' Britain only when Churchill had gambled everything in the hope of American rescue, and allowed

Germany almost to destroy Britain and its Empire.

11. Churchill and the Royal Family worked well and closely together. That was the image created in the second half or the war. But, initially, King George VI opposed the appointment of Churchill, preferred friendship with Germany and hostility to Russia, and favoured a negotiated peace. It is not clear how long those preferences persisted.

12. If Germany had invaded, that would be the end and the British people would have been reduced to slavery. But no invasion of Britain was planned until after Britain had declared war on Germany; even then it might have been just a tactic to divert Russia's attention from the imminent German invasion of Russia. In any case, for those countries that were invaded it was not the end, and they were not reduced to slavery – in Denmark for example.

13. Peace and Appeasement were bad; war was good. Churchill needed or wanted to establish that he and his war (with 'victory') were greater than Chamberlain and his 'Appeasement'. Many people came to think that Appeasement (or even seeking Peace) was discredited. War had won, and many seemed to think that it was a good thing – however much evidence suggested otherwise.

Many myths have grown up about WW2, and need to be challenged. It is worth exploring some generalisations about war. Many of these seem to reflect the reality of WW2; many have more general applicability.

II. Generalisations

1. War inevitably involves costs, including destruction (of homes, infrastructure and so on), injuries and deaths. These should be

carefully considered before any decision to participate is made. There may, or may not, be significant gains for one or more participants. But they may not be worth the human or financial costs involved. Substantial human suffering is unavoidable and the participants often deliberately ignore or try to sidestep this.

2. The results of any war are uncertain, and there are usually unintended consequences. It is therefore not possible to know whether the intended results of a war are worth the costs involved. Some defend Britain's participation in WW2 on the grounds that it was essential to save the Jews, and to prevent Eastern Europe being over-run by a ruthless dictator. But six million Jews perished, and Eastern Europe was over-run by a (different) ruthless dictator. However high-minded the (claimed) intentions may be, the actual consequences of a war are likely to be very different.

3. Before 1914, those who wished to, could go to war in some foreign country and wage war with little or no effect on the people back at home. Since 1914, whole nations have gone to war with serious effects on populations at home including bombing, U-boats and threats to shipping and food supplies. War cannot be regarded as a separate activity for adventurers abroad; there are likely to be many casualties at home.

4. The first casualty in war is Truth. War leaders tend to say whatever they think that they need to say to convince their home populations that they are doing the right thing, that they have a good case for fighting, and that they will win. Their arguments need to be assessed carefully, considering what is really in the national interest, and what is more in the personal interest of the politicians and their supporters.

5. It is rare for one side to be 100% good and right, and for the other

side to be 100% wrong and bad. However, each side's propaganda tends to portray the other side in the worst possible light.

6. Casualties are almost inevitable although euphemisms are used to make light of them (eg 'precision bombing', 'collateral damage' and 'no fly zones'). Each side tends to exaggerate the damage inflicted on the enemy, and to minimise their own casualties. Their numbers should not be taken at face value.

7. The idea of 'total victory', fighting to the death, is problematic. If the enemy is totally humiliated he will bear resentment, and a future national leader is likely to want to redress the balance, or seek revenge, and remove the humiliation, so that his nation can again have self-respect, the respect of others, and be proud and powerful.

8. Most wars end with some sort of negotiated Peace. It would cause much less suffering if Peace were negotiated before and instead of fighting. The 'other side' usually has a reasonably good case, otherwise they would not be able to muster sufficient support to fight. But each side may find it very difficult to understand or accept the other's point of view.

9. There is a tendency to personalise wars, and to characterise the enemy leader as a 'baddie'. However, the underlying causes of wars are more attributable to non-personal factors, such as the (assumed) balance of power, economic resources, pressure from armaments manufacturers, territorial disputes, status and prestige, and avoiding or recovering from, national humiliation.

10. Britain has often refused to negotiate with so-called 'terrorists' and other unsuitable people (for example Nelson Mandela, the Mau Mau in Kenya, and the IRA), but in the end has had to, often after severe fighting. Churchill's refusal to negotiate with Hitler

led to much of the horror of WW2.

11. A country might go to war with honourable intentions, but is often tempted to extreme measures and dishonourable activities in their determination to win. These include invading other countries, use of gas and other weapons of mass destruction, ill-treatment of prisoners of war, bombing and killing innocent women and children.

12. Going to war with a country is likely to make the residents of that country resent or hate their enemy, leading to generations of suspicion, mistrust and future wars. Fighting is likely to make it more difficult to achieve a peaceful settlement with goodwill. V-E Day did not end the fighting between different nationalities in Europe. Hundreds of thousands[228] of people were murdered / executed in the following years. Some were revenge killings of Germans. Old hostilities were revived and reinforced by the war, and are still there today.

13. In WW2, Britain claimed to hold the high moral ground, but it is very difficult to find religious or ethical principles that justify the war.

14. As with many arguments, the more each side attacks the other, the more the other side will fight back, often becoming more extreme in the process.

15. Wars are fought in the interests of different groups at different times. Some people may characterise wars as being led by the ruling classes, with the poor working classes having to work in the factories, fight and die in the interest of their leaders. But in WW2

---

228 For more details see Keith Lowe, *The War Without End,* History Magazine, Aug 2015, p 50-55

Britain, many of the aristocracy and other powerful people were primarily against Russia and communism, and more sympathetic to Germany. But Churchill and others managed to whip up anti-German sentiment, and present the war as a moral crusade. Others talk in terms of the 'national interest', and there is usually a strong element of nationalism in wars, with the 'national interest' being presented as the need to be in control of particular territories, and resources; and national pride. But this ignores the fact that there are many different interest groups in society. Industrialists, such as ship builders, armaments manufacturers, aircraft companies, vehicle makers and many others, can do very well out of a war. Politicians and other leaders (eg Napoleon) have their reputations to consider, sometimes pursuing fame and glory, and having to manoeuvre to obtain and maintain their position. It is worth considering who is more likely to achieve power – the honest peace-loving idealist, or the devious, manipulating nationalist.

There is often substantial opposition to wars (by the people) at first, but eventually most seem to fall into line, and loyally support whatever governments do in their name. Until the advent of modern communications, people had little choice but to believe what their governments and newspapers told them.

Nowadays, people can make up their own minds on the basis of widely available information, and there is often general shock and revulsion when even a small number of people are killed. Governments can no longer get away with the slaughter of hundreds of thousands on some 'moral principle'. But governments' use of propaganda, exaggeration, secrecy and being economical with the truth has not stopped. Each of us should be vigilant and make a stand for peace.

I hope that this book makes some contribution towards people questioning what is done in their name, and in preferring peace and justice to war and violence.

Conclusion

Nearly all British people were very pleased when WW2 ended. They preferred peace to war, and they preferred not to kill and not to be killed. They thought they had experienced Britain's 'finest hour'; all parties had worked together to win the war; Britain had not been invaded; Nazism with all its cruel apparatus had been defeated; Hitler had killed himself; the death camps had been liberated; and the cruelty of the Holocaust had been brought to an end.

British people celebrated. They did not want to be reminded of the horrors and suffering of war. Churchill wrote his account of what had happened, and people believed it. They preferred not to think about anything that could undermine their feelings of self-righteousness. Even seventy years after the war, many people find it too difficult to consider the possibility that Britain might have been wrong to declare war on Germany in 1939, and wrong to continue with it at Britain's weakest hour (May 1940). Although some might find it difficult to challenge conventional assumptions, consideration should be given to the following:

1. Churchill's account was largely an attempt at self-justification. He said himself that it was not history, it was his case – his case for the war that he made his own. He had said that history would be kind to him because he would write it. There was no reason to challenge Churchill's version. The British people could feel good about themselves.

    Part of Churchill's genius was that he

    Constructed brilliant and narrowly plausible narrative for the British people, first about what they might do, and later to persuade them of what they had done[229].

These are the words of a notable supporter of Britain fighting WW2. He does not say:

Churchill told a very clever story, parts of which were believable, in order to convince the British people to fight WW2, and then to convince them that they had done the right thing.

The reader is invited to consider to what extent the two versions differ.

2. Britain had gone to war to help Poland. They did not help Poland. Poland was hopelessly defeated and conquered. Britain's word over Poland was worth no more than Hitler's word over Czechoslovakia.

3. British people liked to think that they had saved the Jews. They did not. Indeed, they made almost no attempt to do so. Six million Jews, and others were murdered. Churchill's priority was winning the war; the Jews were less important; they could wait. The six year wait for most of them meant death. Moreover, Hitler did not invent anti-Semitism. It was widespread throughout Europe, including Britain.

4. Many of the worst features of Nazism were not defeated. Murder of Jews continued (eg in Poland) after the war, and anti-Semitism had not been defeated. Indeed, little or no attempt had been made to address anti-Semitic attitudes, which still exist today.

5. The Nazis conducted cruel experiments on Jews, prisoners and others. That was stopped in Germany, but it seems to

---

229 Hastings, p 661

have inspired similar (though perhaps less cruel) experiments elsewhere. Many dreadful experiments were conducted on humans in England at Porton Down. America conducted many cruel experiments on humans overseas, and in prisons at home. These things are conducted in secret and it is difficult to know how many victims were involved, and exactly what was done to them. But the British government has effectively admitted guilt by paying compensation. The American Government [230]has issued a public apology.

It may be that the Nazis were worse than the Americans or British, but there is no way of knowing, and all such experiments are unacceptable.

It is almost impossible to make governments accountable for what they do in secret. British and American claims to the high moral ground should be taken with a pinch of salt.

6. It is often claimed that Churchill won the war, but no-one knows what he won (apart from fame and glory for himself). There was no invasion of Britain, but none was threatened until after Britain declared war on Germany. Hitler wanted to be left to become some sort of overlord in central and eastern Europe. In return he would leave the British Empire undisturbed.

7. Britain had a responsibility and a duty to protect the citizens of its Empire. They had scarcely enough resources to do so. Instead of fulfilling their responsibilities, Britain engaged in a mad-cap adventure in western Europe, and north Africa supposedly on behalf of Poland, where Britain had no important interest, no military resources, and no prospect of winning.

---

230   President Clinton

8. Russia and America did well out of the war. They won something, whereas Britain did not. Russia came to control most of central and eastern Europe. America developed a massive armaments industry, became Britain's creditor, became virtually the 'overlord' of Britain and its Empire, developed many military bases in different parts of the world and was accepted as a (or the) superpower. Britain became a second class power.

9. The war was hopelessly expensive, and bankrupted Britain. Britain was still paying off its debts more than 50 years later. Britain's infrastructure was neglected for more than five years. Housebuilding stopped and took decades to (temporarily) recover. Ten years after the war bomb damaged buildings were still being rebuilt or replaced. Shortages continued after the war, and food rationing continued for another nine years. Churchill and his government knew that Britain could not finance the war, and desperately gambled that Britain would be rescued by America.

10. Churchill liked to pretend that the war was to save civilisation, democracy and freedom. But his version of civilisation was to advocate a war that killed millions. He suppressed freedom of expression to ensure that his war could be pursued. And he was hardly a democrat[231]. He was a warmonger who wanted fame and glory, and to follow in the footsteps of his illustrious ancestor the Duke of Marlborough. He was desperate to become Prime Minister, and would readily have changed whatever principles he had to achieve that. He would even have accepted office under King Edward VIII to fight on the same side as Germany against Russia and communism.

11. Churchill was not called on by the British people to rescue Britain.

---

231 He did respect Parliament; but he did not respect voters

He manoeuvred himself into the position of Prime Minister, in the teeth of opposition from the King, and most of the Conservative Party. His position became dependent on his continuing the war. The war was more about Churchill's career than it was about principle.

12. Whilst it is clear that the Blitz inflicted huge damage on London and other towns and cities, the British and Americans did far more damage with bombing in Germany, caused far more deaths, and destroyed far more cities. That may in part be because Britain was too weak[232] to fight on land; bombing was much easier.

13. No religious or moral code justifies saturation bombing of cities and of innocent women and children. Yet that was Britain's deliberate policy, and they had planned to do so long before the war.

Britain ...in 1936 had planned a four-engined heavy bomber capable of pulverizing enemy cities into oblivion[233].

The destruction of Dresden by bombing has been much criticised. But the Allies, including Britain, destroyed the heart of many German cities.

The Germans reciprocated – but not until after Britain had started bombing their cities.

14. WW2 had set a dreadful precedent – of dubious legal validity. Hitler's invasion of Poland was of course illegal. Britain helping Poland, particularly at Poland's invitation, would have been legal. The problem was that Britain did not help Poland. Instead Britain

---

232   Britain's army was too small
233   Fischer, p 281

went to war with Germany, to defeat Nazism. Today a war to effect regime change would be illegal without a United Nations resolution supporting it. Unfortunately Britain did not care enough about the League of Nations or about legality.

Fifty or more years after WW2 there are still western powers who feel free to bomb or wage wars to achieve regime change. That is part of WW2's legacy.

15. WW2, in many people's minds, seems to have made war respectable, even glorious and heroic. Many people seem to respect the troops and their murderous endeavours. Patriotism and nationalism, and some of the worst aspects of Nazism, are still strong. Unless people learn to prefer peace and live in co-operation and harmony, nuclear weapons will destroy the world.

Bibliography

Jacob Bannister, *Churchill,* Kindle, 2014

Antony Beevor, *The Second World War,* Weidenfeld and Nicolson, 2012

Patrick J Buchanan, *Churchill, Hitler and the Unnecessary War,* Crown, New York, 2008

Deborah Cadbury, *Princes at War,* Bloomsbury, 2015

Peter Calvocoressi & Guy Wint, *Total War, Causes and Courses of the Second World War, Penguin, 1972*

John Charmley, *Churchill: the End of Glory, a Political Biography,* Hodder and Stoughton, 1993

R Denman, *Missed Chances,* Cassell, 1999

Conan Fischer, *Europe between Democracy and Dictatorship,* Wiley-Blackwell, 2011

Martin Gilbert, *A History of the Twentieth Century,* Harper Collins, 1998

Martin Gilbert (Ed), *Lloyd George,* Prentice Hall, 1968

Charles Higham, *Mrs Simpson: the Secret Lives of the Duchess of Windsor,* Pan, 2005

Adolf Hitler, *Mein Kampf, Jaico, 1988*

Max Hastings, *All Hell Let Loose: the World at War 1939-45, Harper Press, 2011*

Anthony Howard, *RAB, The Life of R A Butler,* Papermac, 1988

Roy Jenkins, *Churchill,* Macmillan, 2001 (Paperback 2002)

Boris Johnson, *The Churchill Factor: How One Man Made History,* Hodder and Stoughton, 2014

Stephen McGinty, *Camp Z: The Secret Life of Rudolf Hess,* Quercus, 2011

Andrew Marr, *A History of Modern Britain,* Macmillan, 2007 (Paperback Pan 2008)

Andrew Morton, *17 Carnations: the Windsors, the Nazis and the Cover-up,* Michael O'Mara Books, 2015

Richard Overy, *The Road to War, the Origins of World War II,* Vintage, 1989

Peter Padfield, *Hess, Hitler and Churchill: The Real Turning Point of the Second World War – A Secret History,* Icon Books, 2014

Lynn Picknett, Clive Prince and Stephen Prior, *War of the Windsors: A Century of Unconstitutional Monarchy,* Mainstream Publishing, Edinburgh, 2002

Lynn Picknett, Clive Prince and Stephen Prior, *Double Standards: The Rudolf Hess Cover Up,* Time Warner, 2001

Clive Ponting, *Churchill,* Sinclair-Stevenson, 1994

Clive Ponting, *1940 Myth and Reality,* Sphere Books, 1990

Andrew Roberts, *Hitler and Churchill: Secrets of Leadership*, Phoenix, 2003

Peter Rowland, *Lloyd George*, Barrie and Jenkins, 1976

Jonathan Schneer, *Ministers at War: Winston Churchill and his War Cabinet*, Oneworld Publications, 2015

Robert Self, *Neville Chamberlain: A Biography*, Ashgate, 2006

W C Sellar and R J Yeatmen, *1066 And All That*, Methuen, 1930

A J P Taylor, *English History 1914-1945*, Oxford History of England, 1965

A J P Taylor, *The Origins of the Second World War*, Penguin Paperback, 1964

Richard Toye, *Lloyd George & Churchill: Rivals for Greatness*, Macmillan, 2007

www.ingramcontent.com/pod-product-compliance
Lightning Source LLC
La Vergne TN
LVHW051255080426
835509LV00020B/2985

9 781910 223659